Git Essentials

Create, merge, and distribute code with Git, the most powerful and flexible versioning system available

Ferdinando Santacroce

PUBLISHING

BIRMINGHAM - MUMBAI

Git Essentials

Copyright © 2015 Packt Publishing

First published: April 2015

Production reference: 1240415

Published by Packt Publishing Ltd.
Livery Place
35 Livery Street
Birmingham B3 2PB, UK.

ISBN 978-1-78528-790-9

www.packtpub.com

Credits

Author
Ferdinando Santacroce

Reviewers
Fabrizio Donina

Giovanni Giorgi

Giovanni Toraldo

Commissioning Editor
Edward Gordon

Acquisition Editor
Meeta Rajani

Content Development Editor
Samantha Gonsalves

Technical Editor
Siddhesh Ghadi

Copy Editors
Hiral Bhat

Karuna Narayanan

Alpha Singh

Project Coordinator
Kinjal Bari

Proofreaders
Simran Bhogal

Safis Editing

Paul Hindle

Bernadette Watkins

Indexer
Tejal Daruwale Soni

Graphics
Jason Monteiro

Abhinash Sahu

Production Coordinator
Nilesh R. Mohite

Cover Work
Nilesh R. Mohite

Foreword

Occasionally, in the IT industry, some inventions are made whose value is far beyond their merely technical merit. Git is one of them.

Git is immensely faster and more convenient than SVN, CVS, and TFS. It is fast becoming the *defacto* standard mainly because there are no tools as powerful and versatile as it is; it is a wonderful masterpiece of code. Behind the success of Git lies much more: it is a revolutionary approach to writing code. Git houses an inherently collaborative component in its DNA. It is no coincidence then that the GitHub's tagline is Social Coding.

If Linus Torvalds goes down in history, it will perhaps be not only for Linux and his genius in writing C, but above all, for the social impact that Git has had on the IT community. Just like the invention of the Web and HTTP have enabled humanity to build a network of communication and collaboration previously unthinkable, Git is the very tool that enables us to transform code development into a social activity. As a matter of fact, Git has started a new era in IT.

Git is also a very well documented tool. If you want to learn the syntax of its 155 commands, you don't need this book; the man pages, which are available for free on the web, are certainly more exhaustive.

However, the heart of Git does not lie in the list of its command options. Just like reading the syntax of the `class` and `interface` keywords will hardly make you grasp the deeper meaning of object-oriented programming, in the same way, the essence of Git won't emerge easily from its man pages.

The hardest part of Git is the paradigm shift that it requires. Honestly, very few books that I've read are able to explain Git and the universe that revolves around it, in a simpler way than the one you're holding in your hands.

This book covers not only all the main topics you can find on the man pages with simplicity and synthesis (such as the commit, stash, rebase, and management of remote), but also has the merit of being one of the few books to give you a 360-degree overview of the ecosystem that every pragmatic programmer should master. It explains how to set up a local server, teaches you the theory and practice behind GitHub and pull requests in a simple and practical way, and even contains a step-by-step guide to migrate from SVN to Git.

Git Essentials has another merit: it is built like a huge tutorial, and is a step-by-step journey through the Git universe. It's not an academic paper; on the contrary, it's full of concrete examples, is written by a programmer, and targeted at other programmers.

It is a book that values code much more than words.

Arialdo Martini

Solutions Architect at Aduno Gruppe

Foreword

At the time of writing this (April 2015), Git has just crossed the historical 10th anniversary since its inception. It is crazy for me to think it's already been 10 years.

Owing not in a small part to the innovative concepts that Git and some earlier DVCS solutions brought about, a huge chunk of the modern software development world has been turned upside down due to it. Teams that have adopted it have been greatly empowered on many fronts.

You can branch off and start working on some experimental features without bothering your colleagues. You can also keep your stable branches stable and only merge completed features. Git will also allow you to explore an entire project while on a plane without sending a single network request.

I went back and looked at my first repository and it appears I started using Git professionally in 2008. Thinking about it, I remember the initial struggle I had with some of the core concepts. Git is not particularly easy to pick up even though its user interface has improved consistently over time.

However, after so many years, we enthusiasts and early adopters have been fooled by our own reality tunnel. It's easy to fall into the perception that nowadays the entire world is already using Git and the transition has been completed. I know for a fact though, that I am mistaken!

During the course of my journey through Europe over the last two years, I have seen teams at all stages of Git adoption. I've noticed, for example, that Nordic countries, such as Sweden and Norway, have been working with Git for several years already, while in other countries, companies have only recently decided to make the transition. It's funny that just a few weeks ago somebody told me that they won't be transitioning to Git any time soon. The reason for this? They spent years migrating from CVS to SVN!

In addition to all that I've said, there is still a pressing need to educate teams all around the world about the usefulness of Git. So, I welcome Ferdinando's work with open arms and his efforts in developing a solid guide for people who want to add Git to their toolkit.

What will you gain from a good understanding of Git? It will forever change the way you write software. You'll be able to save your changes as many times as you want in an unpolished, raw form. You'll also be able to always go back and polish up everything before sharing your work with a rebase.

You will be able to work in isolation on a feature or bug fix without disturbing your teammates or lowering the quality of the master stable branch (refer to *Chapter 2, Git Fundamentals – Working Locally*, for this).

Finally, I can't emphasize enough how Git—and the concepts that are built on it, such as the idea of pull requests—have changed the way professional teams interact, thereby embedding a code review practice into the very texture of the software development process (refer to *Chapter 5, Obtaining the Most – Good Commits and Workflows*).

It's a great time to be adopting Git and reaping the benefits of this solid and efficient tool whether you are a hobbyist or a professional developer. Good luck!

Nicola Paolucci

Developer Advocate at Atlassian

Foreword

Having first used CVS as a source version control more than a decade ago, I remember how easy it was to make the transition to using Subversion, which I thought was all I needed in a source version control tool. Then came Git, Bazaar, and Mercurial, the new kids on the block. I looked at them briefly, but initially, I couldn't see what advantage they could really have for me as a programmer over Subversion, as I was working mostly on my own projects. However, it became more and more evident that to facilitate collaboration, I would have to become much more familiar with these new tools. Very soon it seemed, Git became the first choice and I started using it in earnest. I remember feeling that the tutorials I read seemed needlessly complicated, spending too much time on what I felt were unnecessary details. When I read the first draft of Git Essentials, my first thought was, "This is the book I wish I had when I first learned about Git."

Instead of jumping right away into detailed descriptions of the intricacies of dealing with multiple copies of some software shared by multiple programmers—one of the strengths of distributed source version control software such as Git—Ferdinando Santacroce, the author of Git Essentials, took a different approach, focusing on you first as a potentially lone programmer wishing to use Git.

After going through the basics of installing Git in the first chapter, Ferdinando devotes the following chapter to using it locally, that is, without working with an external repository. This allows you to focus on the basics of Git without the unnecessary complication of dealing with the added concept of an external repository. This is not the way I have seen Git being introduced usually—yet, it is definitely the right way. From this point on, there is a logical progression with important concepts highlighted in a progressive manner. Ferdinando postpones the added complication of working with a remote repository until *Chapter 3, Git Fundamentals – Working Remotely*, using GitHub as an example. Since GitHub has become the most widely used Git repository in the world, this choice is very logical. Yet, the concepts explained in this chapter are just as applicable to other similar sites, such as GitLab or Bitbucket.

There is so much that could be covered when describing how to use Git that it can be a challenge to focus on the essentials, as the title of the book implies. However, Ferdinando has achieved to do just that by making a very judicious use of references to easily accessible external references. The basic topics are well-presented, and pointers to find out more information are added just at the right time. My favorite example of this, which is something I learned from Ferdinando, is to write commit messages before writing the code. Ferdinando mentions this in *Chapter 5, Obtaining the Most – Good Commits and Workflows*, which briefly explains the rationale and includes a reference to a detailed blog post written by Arialdo Martini on this topic. Current Subversion users, who are considering starting using Git, will find *Chapter 6, Migrating to Git*, particularly useful.

Git Essentials is definitely not your traditional dry technical document. Ferdinando's writing style is not only that of a friendly conversation with a friend—one who is passionate about his or her favorite topic and eager to help you learn it—but also that of a friend who knows how to restrain his or her enthusiasm and teach you just enough to enable you to do what you need to do. He does this while giving you useful pointers in case you want to know more.

Dr. André Roberge

Former President and Vice-Chancellor of Université Sainte-Anne

About the Author

Ferdinando Santacroce is a developer, author, and teacher who loves learning new things.

As a software developer, Ferdinando mainly works on the .NET platform using C#, which bridges the gaps between oldstyle systems and new technologies. Over the span of his career, he has allowed COBOL applications to talk with remote services, databases, and electronic devices, such as cash handlers, scanners, and electronic shelf labels. At the moment, he's focusing on continuously improving the Agile Movement, which he follows with great care, in conjunction with XP foundations and lean manufacturing.

While working as a teacher, he developed the first web-based school register in a school of his district, which allowed parents to take a look at grades and absences on a regular basis.

Ferdinando loves to teach people, everyone from children to grandpas, and introduces them to the use of computers, the Internet, and new mobile devices.

He enjoys writing too; after a hiatus of a few years, he started blogging again about his work and passions, which, according to him, is more or less the same thing.

Most of what he's learned over the years has been with the help of his friends and colleagues. This has encouraged him to read books and attend inspiring conferences, such as XP Conference, Italian Agile Day, Codemotion, and others, that help his growth by working on the same code with him.

About the Reviewers

Fabrizio Donina is 34 years old. For 14 years, he worked at a steel plant. He has been involved in the management of industrial automation systems. He first gained experience on platforms, such as Siemens SCADA Cube, Access Database, and Oracle 8i. In recent years, he has had the opportunity to use different development environments, such as SCADA, FactoryTalk by Rockwell, iFix, and WinCC flexible by Siemens. Currently, he's programming PLC Siemens S7 300/400, performing diagnostics and fault searches. Over the years, he has been able to develop software with the help of VB6.0 and Oracle Forms and interface Oracle - > SAP, by implementing Oracle stored procedures for exchanging data. In recent years, he started programming the MES system, which is now in operation at the plant he's working in.

This is the first time he's been asked to review a book. So far, he's always read manuals that have already been published.

I would like to thank Ferdinando Santacroce who got me involved in this great experience.

Giovanni Giorgi is an IT professional with a strong cultural background, and is currently living in Milan, Italy.

Giovanni works for NTT Data and is involved in the IT banking and financial sectors; he's had more then 15 years of experience in Java-based solutions.

Born in 1974, he grew up with Mazinga Z, Daitarn 3, and 8-bit computers by Commodore.

In college, he studied Latin and Greek, along with Turbo Pascal and C programming language as a hobby.

He then started university in September 1993. After one year, he fell in love with the GNU open source philosophy and the Emacs text editor.

Giovanni got a master's degree in information technology from DSI in Milan, Italy, in 2000, and specialized in UML and design pattern integration.

He currently write articles on his blog, which can be found at `http://gioorgi.com`, and you can also find a list of his projects at `https://github.com/daitangio`.

I am grateful to my radiant and beautiful wife, Vanessa Marchiò, who's helped me build a fantastic family, and my two children, Mattia & Sofia; sometimes it's hard to carry on but the reward is always so great.

I would like to thank my strong mother, Mariolga, and my father, Enrico, who've taught me to respect people, to work as a team with others to achieve outstanding results, and also to strongly believe in the concept of justice.

My version of Socrates' daemon started to talk to me when I was eleven, from the creepy circuits of a Commodore VIC-20 with a black and white Philips TV as its monitor.

My little sister, Raffella, was playing printing hearts on that screen but I knew it was my way.

I learned and liked other things, but my passion for information technology will be always part of me; it's similar to an instinct.

"Choose a job you love, and you will never have to work a day in your life."

Giovanni Toraldo started to experiment with Linux and other free software during his early years at school, and he maintained the official Italian support site of PHP-Fusion. After a few unsatisfactory years at the university, he decided to start working as a system administrator and web developer. Now, after having authored a book on OpenNebula, which was released in mid 2012, he works as lead developer for a promising Cloud application marketplace start-up based in Pisa, Italy.

www.PacktPub.com

Support files, eBooks, discount offers, and more

For support files and downloads related to your book, please visit www.PacktPub.com.

Did you know that Packt offers eBook versions of every book published, with PDF and ePub files available? You can upgrade to the eBook version at www.PacktPub.com and as a print book customer, you are entitled to a discount on the eBook copy. Get in touch with us at service@packtpub.com for more details.

At www.PacktPub.com, you can also read a collection of free technical articles, sign up for a range of free newsletters and receive exclusive discounts and offers on Packt books and eBooks.

https://www2.packtpub.com/books/subscription/packtlib

Do you need instant solutions to your IT questions? PacktLib is Packt's online digital book library. Here, you can search, access, and read Packt's entire library of books.

Why subscribe?

- Fully searchable across every book published by Packt
- Copy and paste, print, and bookmark content
- On demand and accessible via a web browser

Free access for Packt account holders

If you have an account with Packt at www.PacktPub.com, you can use this to access PacktLib today and view 9 entirely free books. Simply use your login credentials for immediate access.

Table of Contents

Preface

If you are reading this book, you are probably a software developer and a professional. What makes a good professional? Sure, culture and experience are a part of the answer, but there's more: a good professional is one who can master different tools, choose the best tool for the job at hand, and has the necessary discipline to develop good working habits.

Version control is one of the base skills for developers and Git is one of the right tools for the job. However, Git can't be compared to a screwdriver, a simple tool with only a basic function; Git provides a complete toolbox that can help you manage your own code, within which there are also other sharp tools that should be handled with caution.

The final aim of this book is to help you to start using Git and its commands in the safest way possible, to get things done without causing any injuries. Having said this, you will not get the most from Git commands if you do not acquire the right habits; just as is the case with other tools, in the end, it is the craftsman who makes all the difference.

This book will cover all the basic topics of Git, thereby letting you start using it even if you have little or no experience with versioning systems; you only need to know about versioning in general and the Wikipedia-related page is enough for this purpose.

What this book covers

Chapter 1, *Getting Started with Git* shows you all the (simple) steps you need in order to install Git and do your first commit.

Chapter 2, *Git Fundamentals – Working Locally* reveals the essence of Git, how it takes care of your files, and how you can manage and organize your code.

Chapter 3, Git Fundamentals – Working Remotely moves your attention to the collaborating side of the tool, explaining the basic commands individually and the options you use when working with remote repositories.

Chapter 4, Git Fundamentals – Niche Concepts, Configurations, and Commands completes the basic set of Git commands you need to know, giving you some more weapons to use in difficult situations.

Chapter 5, Obtaining the Most – Good Commits and Workflows gives you some hints about common methods you can use to organize the source code within Git, thereby helping you to develop good habits that every developer should possess.

Chapter 6, Migrating to Git is a way to give you a hand if you're used to other versioning systems, such as Subversion, to manage the transitional phase from another piece of software to Git.

Chapter 7, Git Resources offers you some hints, which I've taken from my experience, and could prove interesting for you.

What you need for this book

To follow the examples used in this book, and make use of them on Git, you only need a computer and a valid Git installation. Git is available for free on every platform (such as Linux, Windows, and Mac OS X). While writing this book, the examples I use are based on the latest version of Git for Windows, which is 1.9.5.

Who this book is for

This book is for developers. The book does not require experience in a particular programming language, nor does it require in-depth experience as a software developer. You can read this book easily if you already use another versioning system, but this can be your first approach to a versioning tool, if you at least know the basics of versioning.

Conventions

In this book, you will find a number of text styles that distinguish between different kinds of information. Here are some examples of these styles and an explanation of their meaning.

Code words in text, database table names, folder names, filenames, file extensions, pathnames, dummy URLs, user input, and Twitter handles are shown as follows: "Go to the local root folder, `C:\Repos`, for the repositories "

Any command-line input or output is written as follows:

```
$ git log --oneline
```

New terms and **important words** are shown in bold. Words that you see on the screen, for example, in menus or dialog boxes, appear in the text like this: " Enabling **Windows Explorer integration** is generally useful."

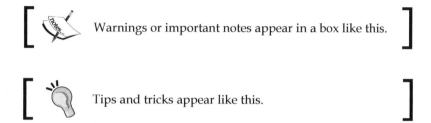

Warnings or important notes appear in a box like this.

Tips and tricks appear like this.

Reader feedback

Feedback from our readers is always welcome. Let us know what you think about this book—what you liked or disliked. Reader feedback is important for us as it helps us develop titles that you will really get the most out of.

To send us general feedback, simply e-mail feedback@packtpub.com, and mention the book's title in the subject of your message.

If there is a topic that you have expertise in and you are interested in either writing or contributing to a book, see our author guide at www.packtpub.com/authors.

Customer support

Now that you are the proud owner of a Packt book, we have a number of things to help you to get the most from your purchase.

Errata

Although we have taken every care to ensure the accuracy of our content, mistakes do happen. If you find a mistake in one of our books—maybe a mistake in the text or the code—we would be grateful if you could report this to us. By doing so, you can save other readers from frustration and help us improve subsequent versions of this book. If you find any errata, please report them by visiting http://www.packtpub.com/submit-errata, selecting your book, clicking on the **Errata Submission Form** link, and entering the details of your errata. Once your errata are verified, your submission will be accepted and the errata will be uploaded to our website or added to any list of existing errata under the Errata section of that title.

To view the previously submitted errata, go to https://www.packtpub.com/books/content/support and enter the name of the book in the search field. The required information will appear under the **Errata** section.

Piracy

Piracy of copyrighted material on the Internet is an ongoing problem across all media. At Packt, we take the protection of our copyright and licenses very seriously. If you come across any illegal copies of our works in any form on the Internet, please provide us with the location address or website name immediately so that we can pursue a remedy.

Please contact us at copyright@packtpub.com with a link to the suspected pirated material.

We appreciate your help in protecting our authors and our ability to bring you valuable content.

Questions

If you have a problem with any aspect of this book, you can contact us at questions@packtpub.com, and we will do our best to address the problem.

1

Getting Started with Git

Whether you are a professional or an amateur developer, you've likely heard about the concept of version control. You may know that adding a new feature, fixing broken ones, or stepping back to a previous condition is a daily routine.

This implies the use of a powerful tool that can help you take care of your work, allowing you to move around your project quickly and without friction.

There are many tools for this job on the market, both proprietary and open source. Usually, you will find **Version Control Systems (VCS)** and **Distributed Version Control Systems (DVCS)**. Some examples of centralized tools are **Concurrent Version System (CVS)**, **Subversion (SVN)**, **Team Foundation Server (TFS)** and **Perforce**, while in DVCS, you can find **Bazaar, Mercurial**, and **Git**. The main difference between the two families is the constraint — in the centralized system — to have a remote server where get and put your files; if the network is down, you are in trouble. In DVCS instead, you can have or not a remote server (even more than one), but you can work offline, too. All your modifications are locally recorded so that you can sync them some other time. Today, Git is the DVCS that has gained public favor more than others, growing quickly from a niche tool to mainstream.

Git has rapidly grown as the de facto to version source code. It is the second famous child of *Linus Torvalds*, who, after creating the **Linux** kernel, forged this versioning software to keep trace of his millions lines of code.

In this first chapter, we will start at the very beginning, assuming that you do not have Git on your machine. This book is intended for developers who never used Git or used it a little bit, but who are scared to throw themselves headlong into it.

If you have never installed Git, this is your chapter. If you already have a working Git box, you can quickly read through it to check whether everything is right.

Installing Git

Git is open source software. If you are running a Windows machine, you can download it for free from `http://git-scm.com`. At the time of writing this book, the current version of Git is 1.9.5. If you are a Mac user, you can download it from `http://git-scm.com/downloads`; here, you can find the `*.dmg` file, too. Finally, if you are a Linux user, you probably have Git out of the box (if not, use the `apt-get install git` command or equivalent). Here, I won't go into too much detail about the installation process itself; I will only provide a few recommendations for Windows users shown in the following screenshot:

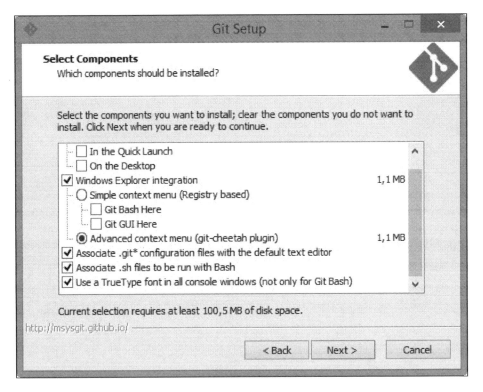

Enabling **Windows Explorer integration** is generally useful; you will benefit from a convenient way to open a Git prompt in any folder by right-clicking on the contextual menu.

Let Git be used in classic DOS command prompt, too, as shown in the following screenshot:

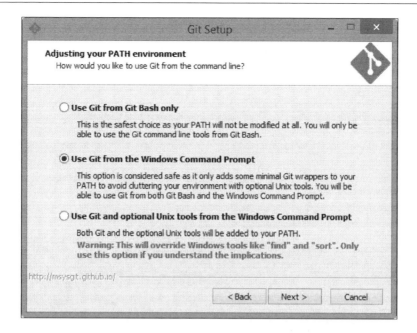

Git is provided with an embedded Windows-compatible version of the famous Bash shell from Linux, which we will use extensively. By doing this, we will also make Git available to third-party applications, such as GUIs and so on. It will come in handy when we give some GUI tools a try.

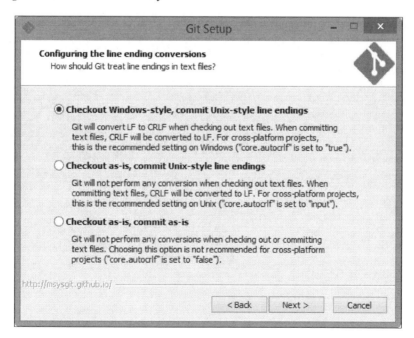

Use defaults for line endings. This will protect you from future annoyances.

At the end of the process, we will have Git installed, and all its *nix friends will be ready to use it.

Running our first Git command

Now, we have to test our installation. Is Git ready to rock? Let's find out!

Open a prompt and simply type `git` (or the equivalent, `git --help`), as shown in the following screenshot:

If Git has been installed correctly, typing `git` without specifying anything else will result in a short help page, with a list of common commands. If not, try reinstalling Git, ensuring that you have checked the **Use Git from the Windows Command Prompt** option. Otherwise, Git will be available only within the embedded Bash shell.

So, we have Git up and running! Are you excited? Let's begin to type!

Setting up a new repository

The first step is to set up a new repository (or repo, for short). A **repo** is a container for your entire project; every file or subfolder within it belongs to that repository, in a consistent manner. Physically, a repository is nothing other than a folder that contains a special `.git` folder, the folder where the magic happens.

Let's try to make our first repo. Choose a folder you like, and type the `git init` command, as shown here:

Whoa! What just happened? Git created a `.git` subfolder. The subfolder (normally hidden in Windows) contains some files and folders, as shown in the next screenshot:

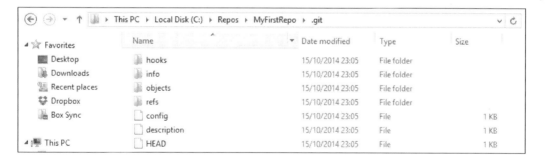

At this point, it is not important for us to understand what is inside this folder. The only thing you have to know is that you do not have to touch it, ever! If you delete it or if you modify files inside by hand, you could get into trouble. Have I frightened you enough?

Now that we have a repo, we can start to put files inside it. Git can trace the history of any gender of files, text based or binary, small or large, with the same efficiency (more or less, large files are always a problem).

Adding a file

Let's create a text file just to give it a try.

And now what? Is that all? No! We have to tell Git to put this file in your repo, *explicitly*. Git doesn't do anything that you don't want it to. If you have some spare files or temp ones in your repo, Git will not be compatible with them, but will only remind you that there are some files in your repo that are not under version control (in the next chapter, we will see how to instruct Git to ignore them when necessary).

Ok, back to the topic. I want `MyFile.txt` under the control of Git, so let's add it, as shown here:

The `git add` command tells Git that we want it to take care of that file and check it for future modifications.

Has Git obeyed us? Let's see.

Using the `git status` command, we can check the status of the repo, as shown in the following screenshot:

As we can see, Git has accomplished its work as expected. In this image, we can read words such as `branch`, `master`, `commit` and `unstage`. We will look at them briefly, but for the moment, let's ignore them.

Commit the added file

At this point, Git knows about `MyFile.txt`, but we have to perform another step to fix the snapshot of its content. We have to commit it using the appropriate `git commit` command. This time, we will add some flavor to our command, using the `--message` (or `-m`) subcommand, as shown here:

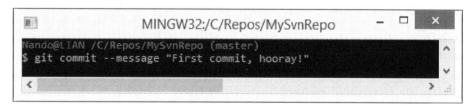

Press the *Enter* key.

Feel the magic—a new branch is born!

With the commit of `MyFile.txt`, we have finally fired up our repo. It now has a `master` branch with a file within it. We will play with branches in the forthcoming chapters. Right now, think of it as a course of our repository, and keep in mind that a repository can have multiple courses that often cross each other.

Modify a committed file

Now, we can try to make some modifications to the file and see how to deal with it in the following screenshot:

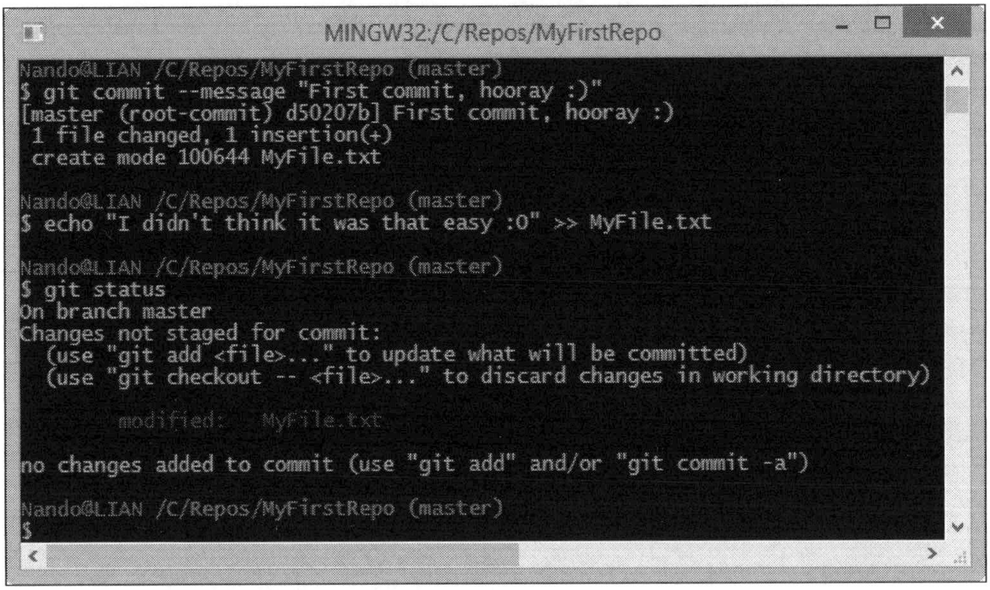

```
MINGW32:/C/Repos/MyFirstRepo                                  _ □ ×

Nando@LIAN /C/Repos/MyFirstRepo (master)
$ git commit --message "First commit, hooray :)"
[master (root-commit) d50207b] First commit, hooray :)
 1 file changed, 1 insertion(+)
 create mode 100644 MyFile.txt

Nando@LIAN /C/Repos/MyFirstRepo (master)
$ echo "I didn't think it was that easy :0" >> MyFile.txt

Nando@LIAN /C/Repos/MyFirstRepo (master)
$ git status
On branch master
Changes not staged for commit:
  (use "git add <file>..." to update what will be committed)
  (use "git checkout -- <file>..." to discard changes in working directory)

        modified:   MyFile.txt

no changes added to commit (use "git add" and/or "git commit -a")

Nando@LIAN /C/Repos/MyFirstRepo (master)
$
```

As you can see, Bash shell warns us that there are some modifications painting the name of the modified files in red. Here, the `git status` command informs us that there is a file with some modifications and that we need to commit it if we want to save this modification step in the repository history.

However, what does `no changes added to commit` mean? It is simple. Git makes you take a second look at what you want to include in the next commit. If you have touched two files but you want to commit only one, you can add only that one.

If you try to do a commit without skipping the `add` step, nothing will happen. We will see this behavior in depth in the next chapter.

So, let's add the file again for the purpose of getting things ready for the next commit.

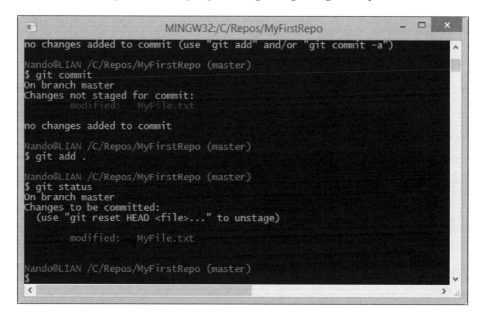

Let's do another commit, this time, avoiding the `--message` subcommand. So, type `git commit` and hit the *Enter* key.

Fasten your seatbelts! You are now entering into a piece of code history!

What is that? It's **Vim (Vi Improved)**, an ancient and powerful text editor. You can configure Git to use your own preferred editor, but if you don't do it, this is what you have to deal with. Vim is powerful, but for newcomers, it can be a pain to use. It has a strange way of dealing with text, so to start typing, you have to press i for inserting text, as shown in the following screenshot:

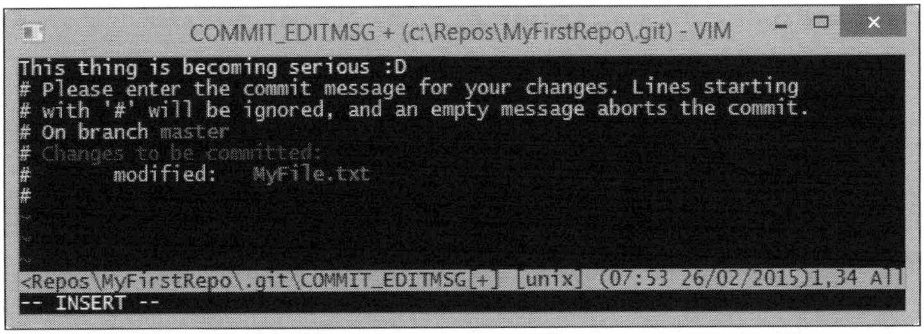

Once you have typed your commit message, you can press *Esc* to get out of the editing mode. Then, you can type the :w command to write changes and the :q command to quit. You can also type the command in pairs as :wq.

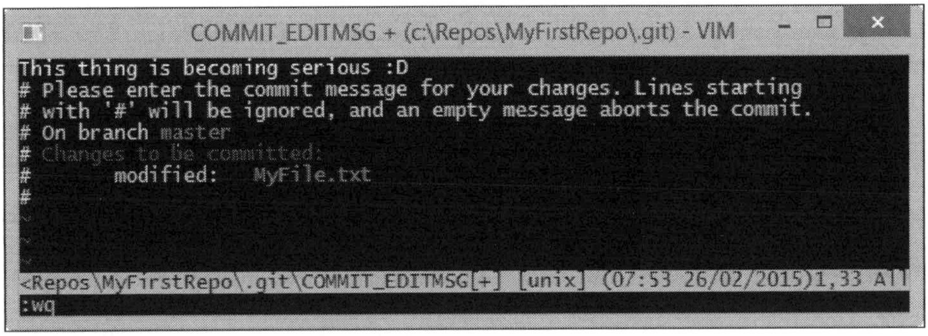

After that, press *Enter* and another commit is done, as shown here:

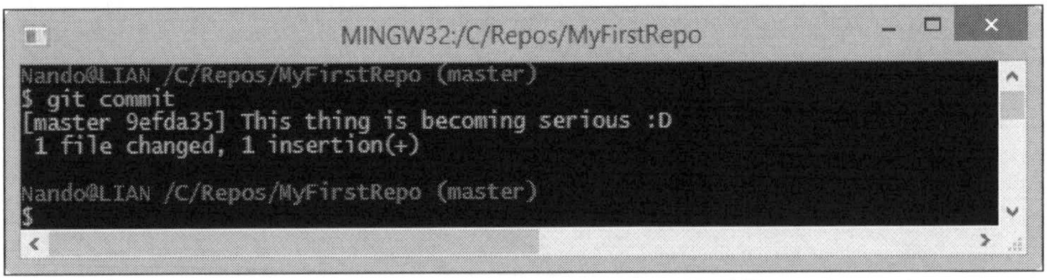

Note that when you saved the commit message in Vim, Git automatically dispatches the commit work, as you can see in the preceding screenshot.

Well done! Now, it's time to recap.

Summary

In this chapter, you learned that Git is not so difficult to install, even on a non-Unix platform such as Windows.

Once you have chosen a directory to include in a Git repository, you can see that initializing a new Git repository is as easy as executing a `git init` command, and nothing more. Don't worry now about saving it on a remote server and so on. It's not mandatory to save it; you can do this when you need to, preserving the entire history of your repo. This is a killer feature of Git and DVCS in general. You can comfortably work offline and push your work to a remote location when the network is available, without hassle.

In the end, we discovered one of the most important character traits of Git: it will do nothing if you don't mention it explicitly. You also learned a little bit about the `add` command. We were obliged to perform a `git add` command for a file when we committed it to Git the very first time. Then, we used another command when we modified it. This is because if you modify a file, Git does not expect that you want it to be automatically added to the next commit (and it's right, I'll say).

In the next chapter, we will discover some fundamentals of Git.

Git Fundamentals – Working Locally 2

In this chapter, we will go deep into some of the fundamentals of Git. It is essential to understand how Git thinks about files, its way of tracking the history of commits, and all the basic commands that we need to master in order to become proficient.

Repository structure and file status life cycle

The first thing to understand while working with Git is how it manages files and folders within the repository. This is the time to analyze a default repository structure.

The working directory

In *Chapter 1, Getting Started with Git*, we created an empty folder and initialized a new repository using the `git init` command (in `C:\Repos\MyFirstRepo`). Starting from now, we will call this folder the **working directory**. A folder that contains an initialized Git repository is a working directory. You can move the working directory around your file system without losing or corrupting your repository.

Within the working directory, you also learned that there is a `.git` directory. Let's call it the **git directory** from now on. In the git directory there are files and folders that compose our repository. Thanks to this, we can track the file status, configure the repository, and so on.

File statuses

In *Chapter 1, Getting Started with Git,* we used two different commands: `git add` and `git commit`. These commands allowed us to change the status of a file, making Git change its status from "I don't know who you are" to "You are in a safe place".

When you create or copy a new file in the working directory, the first state of the file is **untracked**. This means that Git sees that there is something new, but it won't take care of it (it would not track the new file). If you want to include the file in your repository, you have to add it using the `add` command. Once it is added, the state of the file becomes **unmodified**. It means that the file is new (Git says it is unmodified because it never tracked changes earlier) and ready to be committed, or it has reached the **staging area** (also called **index**). If you modify a file that is already added to the index, it changes its status to **modified**.

The following screenshot explains the file status life cycle:

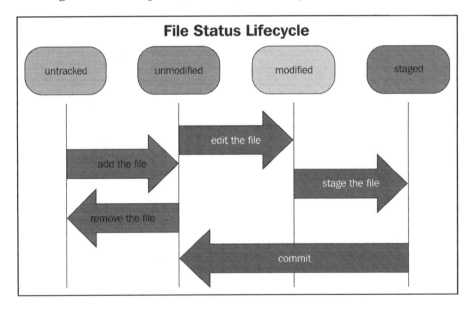

The staging area

The staging area or index is a virtual place that collects all the files you want to include in the next commit. You will often hear people talk about staged files with regard to Git, so take care of this concept. All the files (new or modified) you want to include in the next commit have to be staged using the `git add` command. If you staged a file accidentally, you have to unstage it to remove it from the next commit bundle. Unstaging is not difficult; you can do it in many ways. Let me explain a few concepts. This *several ways to do the same thing* is an organic problem of Git. Its constant and fast evolution sometimes increases confusion, resulting in different commands that do the same thing. This is because it will not penalize people used to working in a particular manner, allowing them the time for some Git revision to understand the new or better way. Fortunately, Git often suggests the best way to do what you want to do and warns you when you use obsolete commands. When in doubt, remember that there are **man pages**. You can obtain some useful suggestions by typing `git <command> --help` (`-h` for short) and seeing what the command is for and how to use it.

Unstaging a file

Well, back to our main topic. Before continuing, let's try to understand the unstaging concept better. Open the repo folder (`C:\Repos\MyFirstRepo`) in Bash and follow these simple steps:

1. Be sure to be in a clean state by typing `git status`. If Git says "nothing to commit, working directory clean," we are ready to start.
2. Create a new file `touch NewFile.txt`.
3. Using `git status` again, verify that `NewFile.txt` is untracked.
4. Add it to the index so that Git can start tracking it. So, use the `git add NewFile.txt` command and go on.

5. When done, use the suggested `git reset HEAD <file>` command to back the file in the untracked status.

It should be clear now. It worked as expected: our file returned in the untracked state, as it was before the `add` command.

`Git reset` is a powerful command, and it can completely destroy your actual work if used improperly. Do not play with it if you don't know exactly what you are doing.

Another way to unstage a file that you just added is to use the `git rm` command. If you want to preserve the file on your folder, you can use the `--cached` option. This option simply removes it from the index, but not from the filesystem. However, remember that `git rm` is to remove files from the index. So, if you use the `git rm` command on an already committed file, you actually mark it for deletion. The next commit will delete it.

The time metaphor

Using the `git reset` command, we also get in touch with another fundamental of Git, the HEAD pointer. Let's try and understand this concept.

A repository is made of commits, as a life is made of days. Every time you commit something, you write a piece of the history.

The past

The past is represented by the previous commits that we did, as shown by **C1** and **C2** in the following diagram:

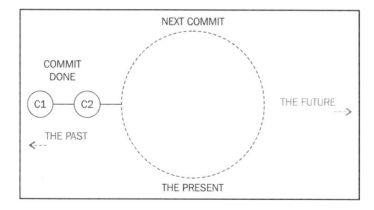

The HEAD pointer is the reference to the last commit we did or the parent of the next commit we will do, as shown in the diagram:

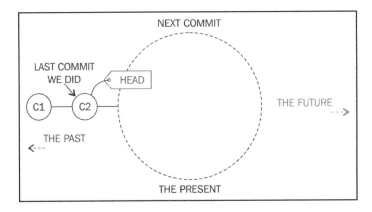

So, the HEAD pointer is the road sign that indicates the way to move one step back to the past.

The present

The present is where we work. When a previous commit is done, it becomes part of the past, and the present shows itself like this diagram:

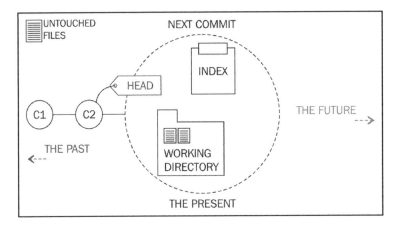

We have a HEAD reference that points out where we came from (the **C2** commit). Resetting to HEAD as we did earlier is a manner of going back in this initial state, where there are no modifications yet. Then, we have the working directory. This directory collects files added to the repository in the previous commits. Now, it is in the untouched state. Within this place, we do our work in files and folders, adding, removing, or modifying them.

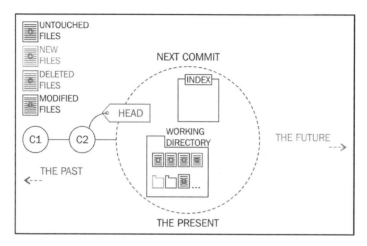

Our work remains in the working directory until we decide to put it in the next commit we will perform. Using the `git add` command, we add what we want to promote to the next commit, marking them into the index, as shown in this diagram:

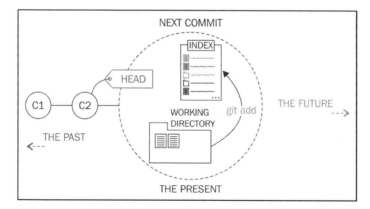

With `git rm --cached <file or folder>`, you can unstage a file by removing it from the index, as shown here:

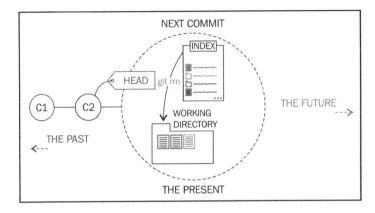

With `git reset --hard HEAD`, we will go back to the initial state, losing all the changes we made in the working directory.

At the end, once you commit, the present becomes part of the past. The working directory comes back to the initial state, where all is untouched and the index is emptied, as shown in this diagram:

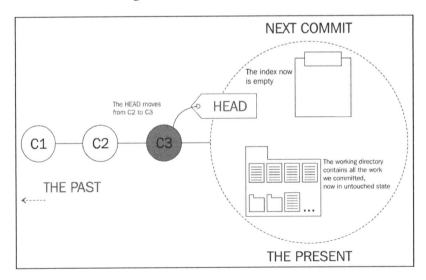

The future

What about the future? Well, even though Git is a very powerful tool, it can't predict the future, not for now at least.

Working with repositories

Let's get our hands dirty!

If you are reading this book, you are probably a programmer, as I am. Using a programming language and its source and binary files to exercise could be fine. However, I don't want to distract you from understanding a language you probably don't use every day. So, let's settle things once and for all. When needed, I will use a nice markup language called **Markdown** (see `http://daringfireball.net/projects/markdown/`).

Apart from being simple yet powerful, Markdown silently became the favorite choice while typing `readme` files (for example, GitHub uses it extensively) or comments in forums or other online discussion places, such as StackOverflow. Mastering it is not our goal, but to be able to do the basic things is surely a skill that can be useful in the future.

Before you proceed, create a new folder for exercises, for example, `C:\Repos\Exercises`. We will use different folders for different exercises.

Unstaging a file

Consider the following scenario. You are in a new repository located in `C:\Repos\Exercises\Ch1-1`. The working directory actually contains two files: `first.txt` and `second.txt`. You have accidentally put both `first.txt` and `second.txt` in the staging area, while you actually want to only commit `first.txt`. So, now:

- Remove the `second.txt` file from the index
- Commit the changes

The result of this is that only `first.txt` will be a part of the commit.

Follow these simple steps to solve this simple task:

1. Create the `C:\Repos\Exercises\Ch1-1` folder and open Bash inside it.

2. Use the `git init` command on the repository as we learned.

3. Create the `first.txt` and `second.txt` files and add them to the staging area, as shown in the following screenshot:

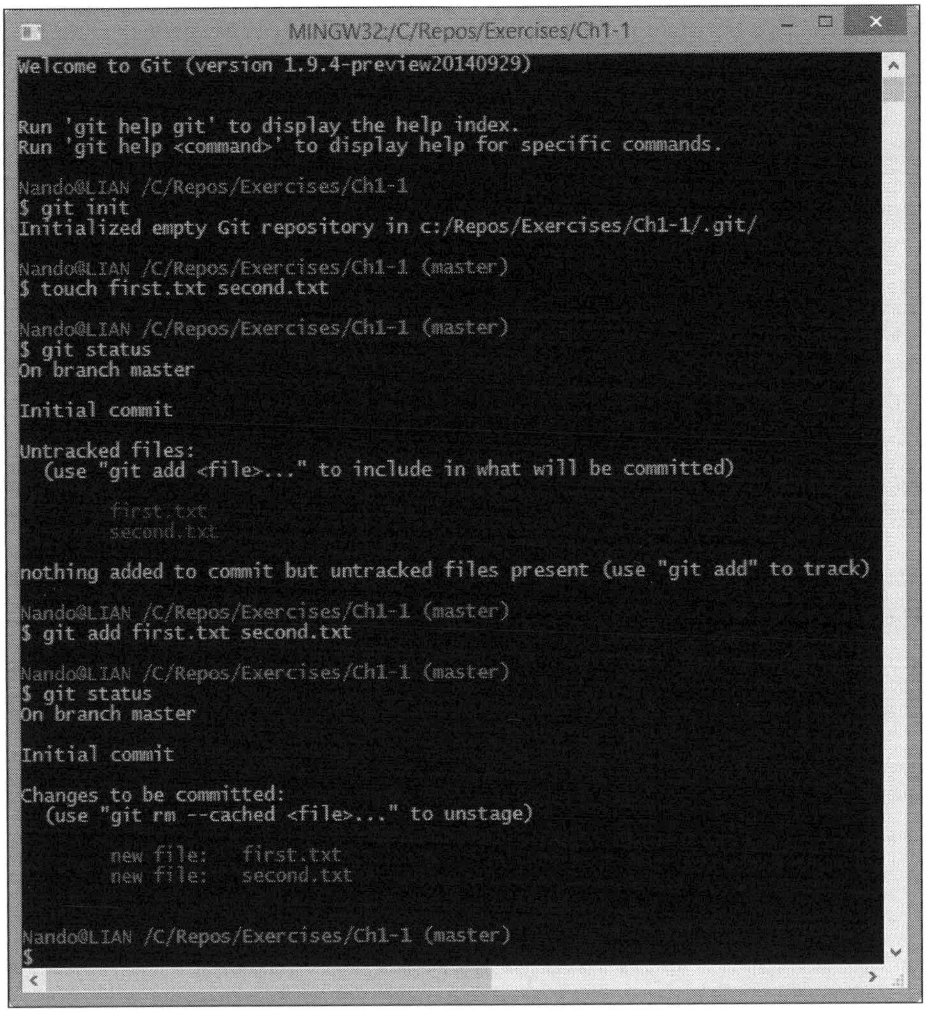

At this point, remove the `second.txt` file and commit. This time, try to use the handy `git rm --cached` command, as suggested here:

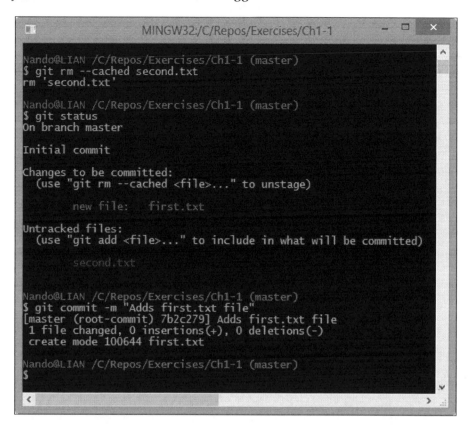

Well done!

Viewing the history

Let's continue where we left off in *Chapter 1, Getting Started with Git*. Walk into
C:\Repos\MyFirstRepo and start a new Bash shell using the right-click shortcut.
Now, use the git log command to see the history of our repository, as shown in
this screenshot:

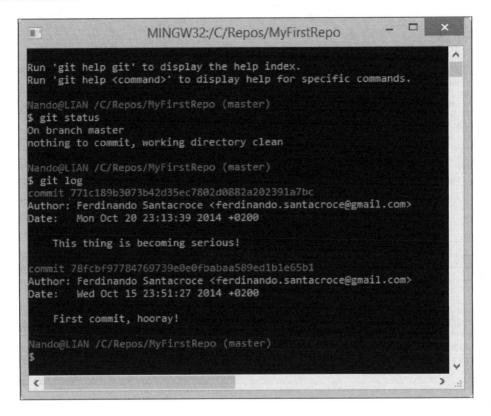

The git log command is very useful and powerful. With this command, we can get
all the commits that we did one by one, each one with its most important details. It's
now time to become more familiar with them.

Anatomy of a commit

Commits are the building blocks of a repository. Every repository is nothing more
than an ordered sequence of commits. If you have a math background, you have
probably already identified an acyclic direct graph in it.

The commit snapshot

Every time we commit something, Git wraps all the files included in a binary blob file. This is one of the most important characteristics of Git. While other versioning systems save files one by one (perhaps using deltas), Git produces a snapshot every time you commit, storing all the files you have included in it. You can assume that a snapshot is a commit, and vice versa.

The commit hash

The commit hash is the 40-character string we saw in logs. This string is the plate of the commit, the way we can refer to it unequivocally. We will not fail to use it in our little exercises.

Author, e-mail, and date

Git is for collaborating, too. So, it is important that every author signs every commit it does to make it clear who did what.

In every commit, you will find the author's friendly name and their e-mail to get in touch with them when necessary. If you are not happy with the actual author you see, change it with the `git config` command, as shown here:

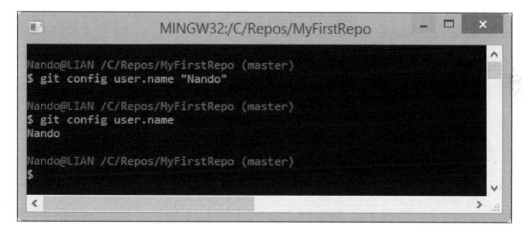

Configuring Git is quite simple. You have to know the name of the object to configure (`user.name` in this example) and give it a `git config <object>` `"<value>"` command. To change the e-mail, you have to change the `user.email` configuration object.

If you want to see the value of an object, simply type `git config <object>` and press *Enter* to get it.

There are three configuration levels: global, user, and repository. We will soon deal with Git configuration in more detail.

Commit messages

In the first chapter, we made two commits, and every time, we added a commit message. Adding a commit message is not only a good practice, it is mandatory. Git would not accept commits without a relative commit message. This is a thing I really appreciate. Let me explain it briefly.

In other versioning control systems, such as SVN, commit messages are optional. Developers, we all know, are lazy people. When they are in a hurry or under stress, the temptation to commit code without telling what feature of the software they are going to add, modify, improve or delete is strong. In no time, you build a mute repository with no change history, and you have to deal with commits that are difficult to understand. In other words, welcome to hell.

Committing a bunch of files

At this point, probably, you are wondering if there is a way to add more than one file at a time. Of course there is! With `git add --all` (`-A`), you add all of the files you have in your working directory to the index. You can also use `<filepattern>` to add only certain types of files; for example, with `git add *.txt`, you can add all text files to the index.

Ignoring some files and folders by default

Often, we work with temp or personal files that we don't want to commit in the repository. So, when you commit all files, it is useful to skip certain kinds of files or folders.

To achieve this result, we can create a `.gitignore` file in the repository. Git will read it and then skip the files and folders we listed inside it.

Let's try to do this in our repository, `C:\Repos\MyFirstRepo`. Perform the following steps:

1. Browse to `C:\Repos\MyFirstRepo`.
2. Create a `.gitignore` file using your preferred editor.

3. Put this text inside it:

```
# === This is a sample of .gitignore file ===
# Ignore temp files
*.tmp
```

4. Save the file.

5. Add the file to the index.

6. Commit the `.gitignore` file.

7. Create a temp file `fileToIgnore.tmp` with a simple `touch` command.

8. Try to add all of the files in your working directory to the index and verify that Git will not add anything.

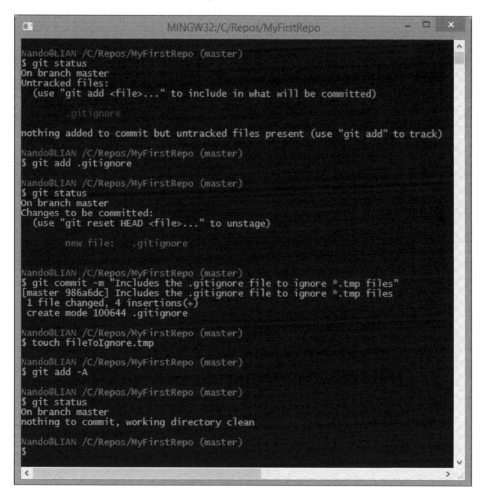

Note that .gitignore file is not retroactive. If you have added some *.tmp files to the index before introducing the .gitignore file, they will stay under revision control. You have to remove them manually if you want to skip them.

The syntax of a .gitignore file is quite simple. Lines starting with # are comments, and they will be ignored. In each line of the file, you can add something to skip. You can skip a single file or folder, certain files by extension, as we did with *.tmp files, and so on.

For the complete syntax of .gitignore see http://git-scm.com/docs/gitignore.

 To add a file in the .gitconfig file even if it is marked to be ignored, you can use the git add -f (--force) option.

Highlighting an important commit – Git tags

We said that commits have an ID and a lot of other useful information bundled with binary blobs of files included. Sometimes, we want to mark a commit with a tag to place a milestone in our repository. You can achieve this by simply using the git tag -a <tag name> command, using -m to type the mandatory message:

```
$ git tag -a MyTagName -m "This is my first tag"
```

Tags will become useful in the future to keep track of important things such as a new software release, particular bug fixes, or whatever you want to put on evidence.

Taking another way – Git branching

Now, it's time to introduce one of the most used features of a versioning system: **branching**. This is a thing that you will use extensively and a thing that Git does well.

Anatomy of branches

A branch is essentially another way your repository takes. While programming, you will use branches to experiment with changes, without breaking the working code. You will use them to keep track of some extensive work, such as the development of a new feature, to maintain different versions or releases of your project. To put it simply, you will use it always.

When in a Git repository, you are always in a branch. If you pay attention to the Bash shell, you can easily find the branch that you are on at the moment. It is always at the prompt, within brackets, as shown here:

The master branch is, conventionally, the default branch. When you do your first commit in a brand new repo, you actually do the first commit in the master branch.

During the course of the book, you will learn that the master branch will often assume an important role. We will only deploy code from that point, and we will never work directly in the master branch.

Looking at the current branches

Let's start using the git branch command alone. If you do this, you will get a list of the branches included in the current repository:

```
$ git branch
```

We will get the following response:

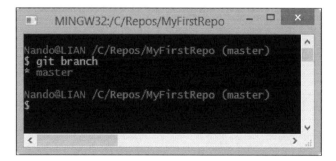

As expected, Git tells us that we have only the master branch. The branch is highlighted with a star and green font just because this is our actual branch, the branch in which we are located at the moment.

Creating a new branch

Now, let's start creating a new branch for a new activity.

Open the Bash shell in `C:\Repos\MyFirstRepo` and create a new branch from where you are using the `git branch` command, followed by the name of the branch we want to create. Let's assume that the name of the branch is `NewWork`:

```
$ git branch NewWork
```

Well, it seems nothing happened and we are still in the `master` branch as we can see in the following screenshot:

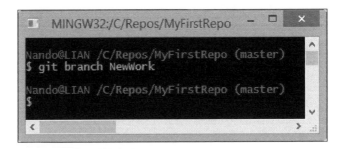

Git sometimes is a man of few words. Type the `git branch` command again to get a list of the actual branches:

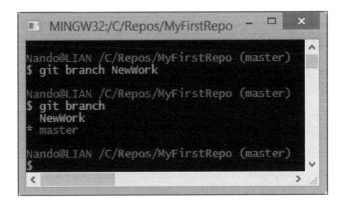

Hey, there's a `NewWork` branch now!

Switching from branch to branch

The only thing we have to do now is to switch to the NewWork branch to begin working on this separate argument. To move around from one branch to another, we will use the git checkout command. Type this command followed by the branch name to switch to:

```
$ git checkout NewWork
```

This time, Git gave us a short message, informing us that we have switched to the NewWork branch. As you can see, NewWork is within brackets in place of master, indicating the actual branch to us:

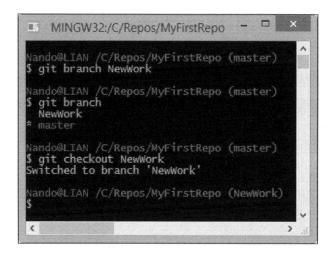

Super easy, isn't it?

Understanding what happens under the hood

At this point, nothing special seems to have happened. However, you will soon change your mind. Just to give you a visual aid, consider this figure:

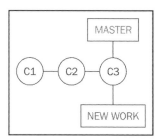

Assume that our last commit on the `master` branch was the **C3** commit. At this point, we now have two other pointers: the `master` branch pointer and the `NewWork` branch pointer.

If you have used Subversion or a similar versioning system earlier, at this point, you would probably look for a `NewWork` folder in `C:\Repos\MyFirstRepo`. However, unfortunately, you will not find it. Git is different, and now, we will see why.

Now, to better understand what a branch is for, add `NewWorkFile.txt`, stage it, and commit the work, as shown here:

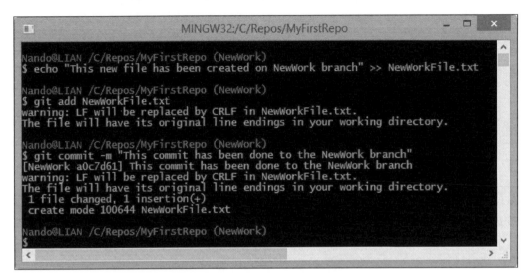

At this point, we have a new commit in the `NewWork` branch. This commit is not a part of the `master` branch, because it has been created in another branch. So, the `NewWork` branch is ahead of the `master` branch, as shown in the following figure:

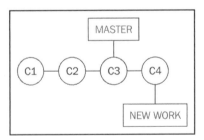

Working with Git in this kind of a situation is ordinary administration, just like it is in the day-to-day life of a developer. Creating a new branch is cheap and blazing fast even in large repositories, because all the work is done locally. You can derive multiple branches from a unique point, branch from a branch that branched into another branch, and so on, creating all the ramifications you can manage without going crazy.

Moving from a branch to another is easy. So, let's turn back to the master branch and see what happens:

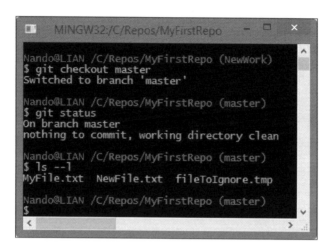

If you have used Subversion earlier, at this time, you are probably wondering at least two things: why is there no NewWork folder containing files from that branch and, most of all, what was the fate of the NewWorkFile.txt file.

In **Apache Subversion (SVN)**, every branch (or tag) you checked out resides in a separate folder (bloating your repository, after some time). In Git, there is a huge difference. Every time you check out a branch, files and folders of the previous branch are replaced with those contained in the new branch. Files and folders only on the destination branch are restored, and those only on the previous branch are deleted. Your working directory is constantly a mirror of the actual branch. To have a look at another branch, you basically have to switch to it.

This aspect might look bad to you the first time, because seeing files and folders disappear is scary at first. Then, you can't differentiate the two branches as we probably did earlier by simply comparing the content of the two folders with your preferred tool. If I can give you a piece of advice, don't lose heart about this (as I did at the beginning): soon you will forget what you lost and you will fall in love with what you gained.

A bird's eye view to branches

So, let's go back once again to the NewWork branch and have a look at the situation with the aid of a visual tool, Git GUI. Open the C:\Repos\MyFirstRepo folder and right-click inside it. Choose **Git GUI** from the contextual menu. A dialog box will pop up as shown in the following screenshot:

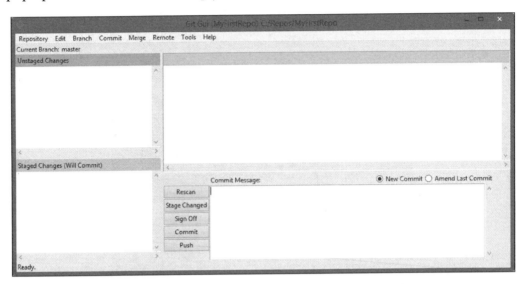

Git GUI is not my preferred GUI tool, but you have it for free when installing Git. So, let's use it for the moment.

Go to **Repository | Visualize All Branch History**. A new window will open, and you will see the status of our current branches, as shown in the following screenshot:

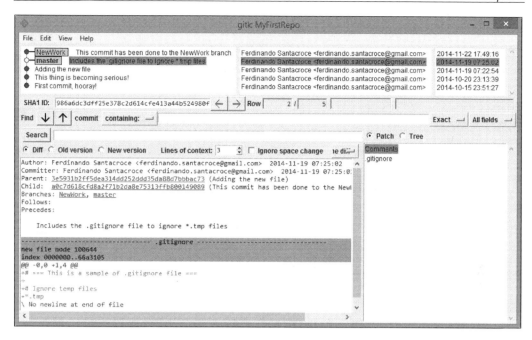

We do not have the time to go into all the details here. As you become more confident with Git fundamentals, you will learn little by little all the things you see in the preceding picture.

If you don't want to leave the console to take a look, you could get a pretty output log even on the console. Try this articulated `git log` command:

```
$git log --graph --decorate --pretty=oneline --abbrev-commit
```

This is a more compact view, but it is as clear as what we saw earlier.

Typing is boring – Git aliases

Before continuing, just a little warning. The last command we used is not the easiest thing to remember. To get around this nuisance, Git offers the possibility of creating your own commands, aliasing some of the verbose sequences.

To create an alias, we will use the `git config` command. So, let's try to create a `tree` alias for this command:

```
$ git config --global alias.tree 'log --graph --decorate --pretty=oneline
--abbrev-commit'
```

So, the syntax to create aliases is as follows:

```
git config <level> alias.<alias name> '<your sequence of git commands>'
```

Using the `--global` option, we told Git to insert this alias at the user level so that any other repository for my user account on this computer will have this command available. We have three levels where we can apply config personalization:

- Repository level configs are only available for the current repo
- Global configs are available for all the repos for the current user
- System configs are available for all the users/repositories

To create a repository user-specific config, we used the `--global` option. For the system level, we will use the `--system` option. If you don't specify any of these two options, the config will take effect only in the repository that you are in now.

Merging branches

Now that we finally got in touch with branches, let's assume that our work in the NewWork branch is done and we want to bring it back to the master branch.

To merge two branches, we have to move to the branch that contains the other branch commits. So, if we want to merge the NewWork branch into the master branch, we would first have to check out the master branch. As seen earlier, to check out a branch we have to type the following command:

```
$ git checkout <branch name>;
```

If you want to check out the previous branch you were in, it's even simpler. Type this command:

```
$ git checkout -
```

With the git checkout - command, you will move in the previous branch without having to type its name again as explained in the following screenshot:

Now, let's merge the NewWork branch into master using the git merge command:

```
$ git merge NewWork
```

As you can see, merging is quite simple. With the `git merge <branch to merge>` command, you can merge all the modifications in a branch into the actual branch as shown in the following screenshot:

```
MINGW32:/C/Repos/MyFirstRepo                      –  □  ×
Nando@LIAN /C/Repos/MyFirstRepo (master)
$ git merge NewWork
Updating 986a6dc..a0c7d61
Fast-forward
 NewWorkFile.txt | 1 +
 1 file changed, 1 insertion(+)
 create mode 100644 NewWorkFile.txt

Nando@LIAN /C/Repos/MyFirstRepo (master)
$
```

When we read console messages, we see that Git is telling us something interesting. Let's take a look.

When Git says `Updating 986a6dc..a0c7d61`, it is telling us that it is updating pointers. So now, we will have `master`, `NewWork`, and `HEAD` all pointing to the same commit:

```
MINGW32:/C/Repos/MyFirstRepo                      –  □  ×
Nando@LIAN /C/Repos/MyFirstRepo (master)
$ git tree
* a0c7d61 (HEAD, master, NewWork) This commit has been done to the NewWork branch
* 986a6dc Includes the .gitignore file to ignore *.tmp files
* 3e5931b Adding the new file
* 771c189 This thing is becoming serious!
* 78fcbf9 First commit, hooray!

Nando@LIAN /C/Repos/MyFirstRepo (master)
$
```

`Fast-forward` is a concept that we will cover soon. When we tell Git to not apply this feature, in brief, this fast-forward feature (enabled by default) permits us to merge commits from different branches, as they were done subsequently in the same branch, obtaining a less-pronged repository.

Last, but not least, we have a complete report of what files are added, deleted, or modified. In our case, we had just one change (an insertion) and nothing else. When something is added, Git uses a green plus symbol +. When a deletion happens, Git uses a red dash symbol -.

Merge is not the end of the branch

This is a concept that sometimes raises some trouble. To avoid this, we will have a quick glimpse of it. You don't have to wait for the work to be done before merging another branch into your branch. Similarly, you don't have to think about merging as the last thing you will do before cutting off the other branch on which you worked.

On the contrary, it's better if you merge frequently from branches you depend on, because doing it after weeks or months can become a nightmare: too many changes in the same files, too many additions or deletions. Don't make a habit of this!

Exercises

To understand some common merging scenarios, you can try to resolve these small exercises.

Exercise 2.1

In this exercise we will learn how Git can handle automatically file modifications when they are not related to the same lines of text.

What you will learn

Git is able to automerge modifications on the same files.

Scenario

1. You are in a new repository located in `C:\Repos\Exercises\Ch2-1`.
2. You have a `master` branch with two previous commits: the first commit with a `file1.txt` file and the second commit with a `file2.txt` file.
3. After the second commit, you created a new branch called `File2Split`. You realized that `file2.txt` is too big, and you want to split its content by creating a new `file2a.txt` file. Do it, and then commit the modifications.

Results

Merging back `File2Split` in the `master` branch is a piece of cake. Git takes care of deletion in `file2.txt` without spotting your conflicts.

Exercise 2.2

In this exercise we will learn how to resolve conflicts when Git cannot merge files automatically.

What you will learn

Git will result in conflicts if automerging is not possible.

Scenario

1. You are in the same repository used earlier, `C:\Repos\Exercises\Ch2-1`.

2. On the `master` branch, you add the `file3.txt` file and commit it.

3. Then, you realize that it is better to create a new branch to work on `file3.txt`, so you create the `File3Work` branch. You move in this branch, and you start to work on it, committing modifications.

4. The day after, you accidentally move to the `master` branch and make some modifications on the `file3.txt` file, committing it.

5. Then, you try to merge it.

Results

Merging the `File3Work` branch in `master` gives rise to some conflicts. You have to solve them manually and then commit the merged modifications.

Deal with branches' modifications

As mentioned earlier, if you come from SVN at this point, you would be a little confused. You don't "physically have on the disk" all the branches checked out on different folders. Because of this, you cannot easily differentiate two branches to take into account what a merge will cost in terms of conflicts to resolve.

Well, for the first problem, there is not an SVN-like solution. However, if you really want to differentiate two checked out branches, you could copy the working directory in a `temp` folder and check out the other branch. This is just a workaround, but the first time can be a less traumatic way to manage the mental shift Git applies in this field.

Diffing branches

If you want to do it in a more Git-like way, you could use the `git diff` command. Let's give it a try by performing the following steps:

1. Open `C:\Repos\MyFirstRepo` and switch to the `master` branch.

2. Add some text to the existing `NewFile.txt`, and then save it.

3. Add a `NewMasterFiles.txt` file with some text within it. At the end, add both files to the index and then commit them, as shown in the following screenshot:

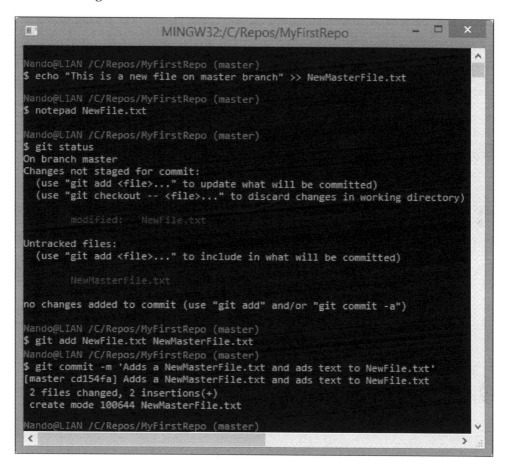

Now, try to have a look at the differences between the `master` and `NewWork` repositories. Finding out the difference between the two branches is easy with the `git diff` command:

```
$ git diff master..NewWork
```

The syntax is simple: `git diff <source branch>..<target branch>`. The result, instead, is not probably the clearest thing you have ever seen:

```
Nando@LIAN /C/Repos/MyFirstRepo (master)
$ git diff master..NewWork
diff --git a/NewFile.txt b/NewFile.txt
index 0ae6d47..e69de29 100644
--- a/NewFile.txt
+++ b/NewFile.txt
@@ -1 +0,0 @@
-Added some text to the existing NewFile
\ No newline at end of file
diff --git a/NewMasterFile.txt b/NewMasterFile.txt
deleted file mode 100644
index 679667b..0000000
--- a/NewMasterFile.txt
+++ /dev/null
@@ -1 +0,0 @@
-This is a new file on master branch
```

However, with a little imagination, you can understand that the differences are described from the point of view of the `NewWork` branch. Git is telling us that some things on `master` (`NewFile.txt` modifications and `NewMasterFile.txt`) are not present in the `NewWork` branch.

If we change the point of view, the messages change to those shown in the following screenshot:

```
Nando@LIAN /C/Repos/MyFirstRepo (master)
$ git diff NewWork..master
diff --git a/NewFile.txt b/NewFile.txt
index e69de29..0ae6d47 100644
--- a/NewFile.txt
+++ b/NewFile.txt
@@ -0,0 +1 @@
+Added some text to the existing NewFile
\ No newline at end of file
diff --git a/NewMasterFile.txt b/NewMasterFile.txt
new file mode 100644
index 0000000..679667b
--- /dev/null
+++ b/NewMasterFile.txt
@@ -0,0 +1 @@
+This is a new file on master branch
```

To better understand these messages, you can take a look at the diff output at `http://en.wikipedia.org/wiki/Diff_utility`.

Another way to check differences is to use `git log`:

```
$ git log NewWork..master
```

This command lets you see commits that differ from the NewWork branch to the master branch.

There is even a `git shortlog` command to give you a more compact view, as shown in the following screenshot:

```
Nando@LIAN /C/Repos/MyFirstRepo (master)
$ git log NewWork...master
commit cd154fae66f188c33b2f5e48b68dead989ed7187
Author: Ferdinando Santacroce <ferdinando.santacroce@gmail.com>
Date:   Sun Nov 23 18:47:39 2014 +0100

    Adds a NewMasterFile.txt and ads text to NewFile.txt

Nando@LIAN /C/Repos/MyFirstRepo (master)
$ git shortlog NewWork...master
Ferdinando Santacroce (1):
      Adds a NewMasterFile.txt and ads text to NewFile.txt
```

Using a visual diff tool

All these commands are useful for short change history. However, if you have a more long change list to scroll, things would quickly become complicated.

Git lets you use an external diff tool of choice. On other platforms (for example, Linux or Mac), a diff tool is usually present and configured, while on the Windows platform, it is generally not present.

To check this, type this command:

```
$ git mergetool
```

If you see a message like this, you would probably have to set your preferred tool:

```
Nando@LIAN /C/Repos/MyFirstRepo (master)
$ git mergetool

This message is displayed because 'merge.tool' is not configured.
See 'git mergetool --tool-help' or 'git help config' for more details.
'git mergetool' will now attempt to use one of the following tools:
tortoisemerge emerge vimdiff
No known merge tool is available.
```

Resolving merge conflicts

As we have seen, merging branches is not a difficult task. However, in real-life scenarios, things are not that easy. We have conflicts, modifications on both branches, and other weird things to fight. In this section, we will take a look at some of them. However, first, remember one important thing: it needs a little bit of discipline to make the most of Git.

You have to avoid at least two things:

- Working hard on the same files on different branches
- Rarely merging branches

Edit collisions

This is the most common kind of conflict: someone edited the same line in the same file on different branches, so Git can't auto merge them for you. When this happens, Git writes special conflict markers to the affected areas of the file. At this point, we have to manually solve the situation, editing that area to fit our needs.

Let's try this by performing the following steps:

1. Open your repository located in C:\Repos\MyRepos.
2. Switch to the NewWork branch and edit NewFile.txt by modifying the first line Added some text to the existing NewFile in Text has been modified.
3. Add and commit the modification.

4. Switch back to `master` and merge the `NewWork` branch.

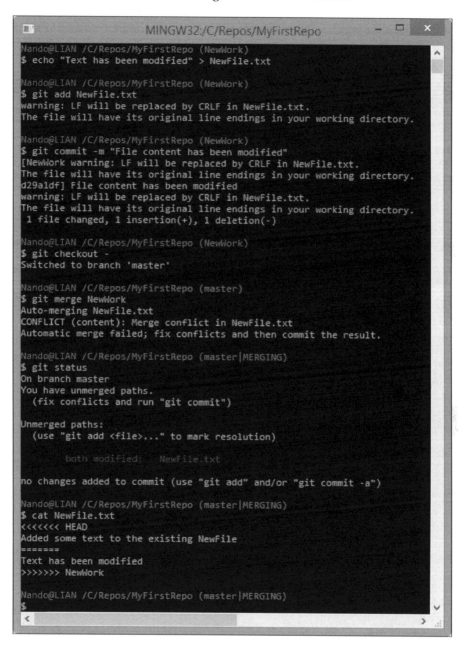

As you can see, Git highlighted the conflict. A conflict-marked area begins with <<<<<< and ends with >>>>>>>. The two conflicting blocks themselves are divided by a sequence of =======. To solve the conflict, you have to manually edit the file, deciding what to maintain, edit, or delete. After that, remove the conflict markers and commit changes to mark the conflict as resolved.

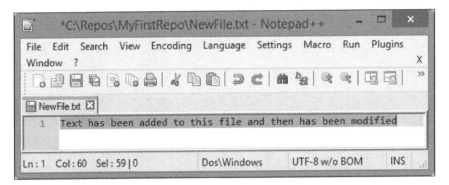

Once you resolve the conflicts, you are ready to add and commit:

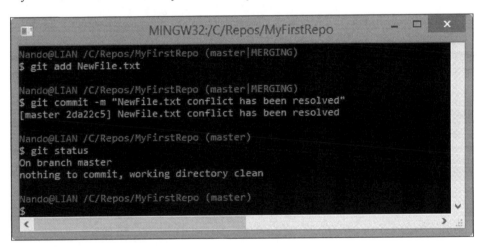

Merge done, congratulations!

Resolving a removed file conflict

Removed file conflicts occur when you edit a file in a branch and another person deletes that file in their branch. Git does not know if you want to keep the edited file or delete it, so you have to take the decision. This example will show you how to resolve this both ways.

Keeping the edited file

Try again using NewFile.txt. Remove it from the NewWork branch and then modify it in master:

After that, merge `NewWork` in the `master` branch. As said earlier, Git spots a conflict. Add `NewFile.txt` again in the `master` branch and commit it to fix the problem:

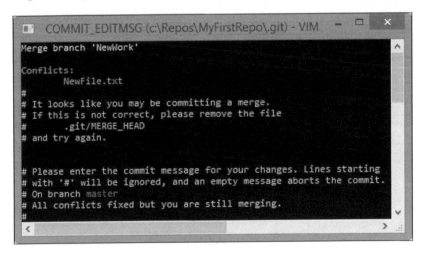

When resolving merge conflicts, try to commit without specifying a message, using only the `git commit` command. Git will open the Vim editor, suggesting a default merge message:

This can be useful to spot merge commits looking at the repository history in the future.

Resolving conflicts by removing the file

If you agree with the deletion of the file in the other branch, instead of adding it again, remove it from your branch. So, use the `git rm NewFile.txt` command even in the `master` branch and then commit to mark the conflict resolved.

Stashing

Working of different features in parallel does not make a developer happy, but sometimes it happens. So, at a certain point, we have to break the work on a branch and switch to another one. However, sometimes, we have some modifications that are not ready to be committed, because they are partial, inconsistent, or even won't compile. In this situation, Git prevents you from switching to another branch. You can only switch from one branch to another if you are in a clean state:

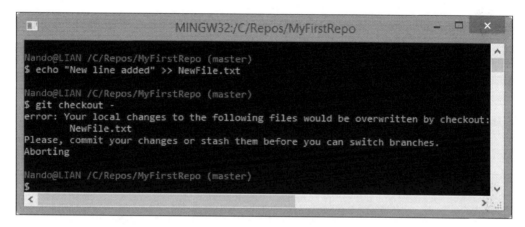

To quickly resolve this situation, we can stash the modifications, putting them into a sort of box, ready to be unboxed at a later time.

Stashing is as simple as typing the `git stash` command. A default description will be added to your stash, and then modifications will be reverted to get back in a clean state:

To list actual stashes, you can use the `list` subcommand:

Once you have done the other work, you can go back to the previous branch and apply the stash to get back to the previous "work in progress" situation:

```
                    MINGW32:/C/Repos/MyFirstRepo          —   □   ×
Nando@LIAN /C/Repos/MyFirstRepo (master)
$ git stash apply
On branch master
Changes not staged for commit:
  (use "git add <file>..." to update what will be committed)
  (use "git checkout -- <file>..." to discard changes in working directory)

        modified:   NewFile.txt

no changes added to commit (use "git add" and/or "git commit -a")

Nando@LIAN /C/Repos/MyFirstRepo (master)
$
```

What we have seen is the most common scenario and most used approach, but stashing is a powerful Git tool. You can have multiple stashes, apply a stash to a different branch, or reverse apply a stash. You can even create a branch starting from a stash. You can learn more about this on your own.

Summary

In this chapter, you learned the core concepts of Git: how it handles files and folders, how to include or exclude files in commits that we do, and how commits compose a Git repository.

Next, we explored the most used and powerful feature of Git, its ability to manage multiple parallel branches. For a developer, this is the feature that saves you time and headache while working on different parts of your project. This feature lets you and your colleagues collaborate without conflicts.

At the end, we touched on Git's stashing ability, where you can freeze your current work without having to commit an unfinished change. This helps you develop good programmer habits, such as the one that tells you to not commit an unfinished change.

In the next chapter, we will complete our journey of Git fundamentals, exploring ways and techniques to collaborate with other people.

3
Git Fundamentals – Working Remotely

In this chapter, we will finally start to work in a distributed manner, using remote servers as a contact point for different developers. As we said earlier, Git is a distributed version-control system. This chapter is for the distributed part.

Working with remotes

You know that Git is a tool for versioning files. However, it has been built with collaboration in mind. In 2005, Linus Torvalds had the need for a light and efficient tool to handle tons of patches proposed to the Linux kernel from a multitude of contributors. He wanted a tool that would allow him and hundreds of other people to work on it without going crazy. The pragmatism that guided its development gave us a very robust layer to share data among computers, without the need of a central server.

A Git remote is another computer that has the same repository you have on your computer. Every computer that hosts the same repository on a shared network can be the remote of other computers:

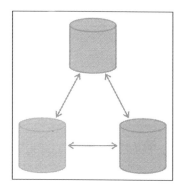

So, a remote Git repository is nothing other than a remote copy of the same Git repository we created locally. If you have access to that host via common protocols such as SSH, HTTPS or the custom git:// protocol, you can keep your modification with it in sync.

The great difference between Git and other **distributed version control systems (DVCS)** to classical centralized versioning systems (VCS) such as Subversion is that there's no central server where you can give custody of your repository. However, you can have many remote servers. This allows you to be fault tolerant and have multiple working copies where you can get or pull modifications, giving you incredible flexibility.

To start working with a remote, we have to get one. Today, it is not difficult to get a remote. The world has plenty of free online services that offer room for Git repositories. One of the most commonly used repository is **GitHub**. Before starting, note that GitHub offers free space for open source repositories, so everyone in the world can access their code. Be careful, and don't store sensitive information such as passwords and so on in your repository; they will be publicly visible.

Setting up a new GitHub account

GitHub offers unlimited free public repositories, so we can make use of them without investing a penny. In GitHub, you have to pay only if you need private repositories, for example, to store the closed source code on which you base your business.

Creating a new account is simple. Just perform the following steps:

1. Go to `https://github.com`.
2. Sign up using your e-mail.

When done, we are ready to create a brand new repository where we can push our work:

Go to the **Repositories** tab, click on the green **New** button, and choose a name for your repository:

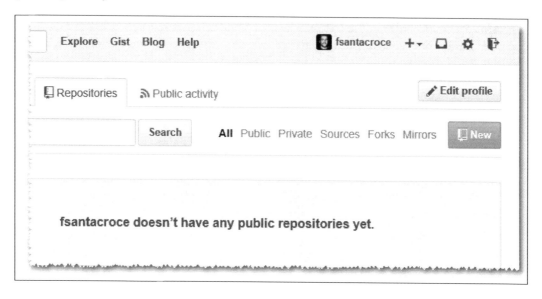

For the purpose of learning, I will create a simple repository for my personal recipes. These recipes are written using the Markdown markup language (http://daringfireball.net/projects/markdown/).

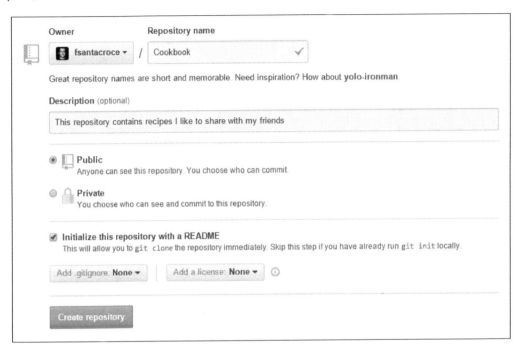

Then, you can write a description for your repository. This is useful to allow people who come to visit your profile to better understand what your project is intended for. We create our repository as public because private repositories have a cost, as we said earlier. Then, we initialize it with a README file. Choosing this GitHub makes a first commit for us, initializing the repository that is now ready to use.

Cloning a repository

Now, we have a remote repository, so it's time to learn how to hook it locally. For this, Git provides the `git clone` command.

Using this command is quite simple. All we need to know is the URL of the repository to clone. The URL is provided by GitHub in the bottom-right corner of the repository home page, as shown in the following screenshot:

To copy the URL, you can simply click on the clipboard button on the right-hand side of the textbox.

So, let's try to follow these steps together:

1. Go to the local root folder, `C:\Repos`, for the repositories.

2. Open a Bash shell within it.

3. Type `git clone https://github.com/fsantacroce/Cookbook.git`.

Obviously, the URL of your repository will be different. As you can see in this screenshot, GitHub URLs are composed by `https://github.com/<Username>/<RepositoryName>.git`:

```
MINGW32:/C/Repos/Cookbook
Welcome to Git (version 1.9.5-preview20141217)


Run 'git help git' to display the help index.
Run 'git help <command>' to display help for specific commands.

Nando@LIAN /C/Repos
$ git clone https://github.com/fsantacroce/Cookbook.git
Cloning into 'Cookbook'...
remote: Counting objects: 3, done.
remote: Compressing objects: 100% (2/2), done.
remote: Total 3 (delta 0), reused 0 (delta 0)
Unpacking objects: 100% (3/3), done.
Checking connectivity... done.

Nando@LIAN /C/Repos
$ ls -l
total 6
drwxr-xr-x    4 Nando    Administ        0 Dec 21 17:16 Cookbook
drwxr-xr-x    9 Nando    Administ    12288 Nov 30 16:02 MyFirstRepo

Nando@LIAN /C/Repos
$ cd Cookbook/

Nando@LIAN /C/Repos/Cookbook (master)
$
```

At this point, Git created a new `Cookbook` folder that contains the downloaded copy of our repository. Inside, we will find a `README.md` file, a classical one for a GitHub repository. In this file, you can describe your repository using the common Markdown markup language to users who will chance upon it.

Uploading modifications to remotes

So, let's try to edit the `README.md` file and upload modifications to GitHub:

1. Edit the `README.md` file using your preferred editor. You can add, for example, a new sentence.

2. Add it to the index and then commit.

3. Put your commit on the remote repository using the `git push` command.

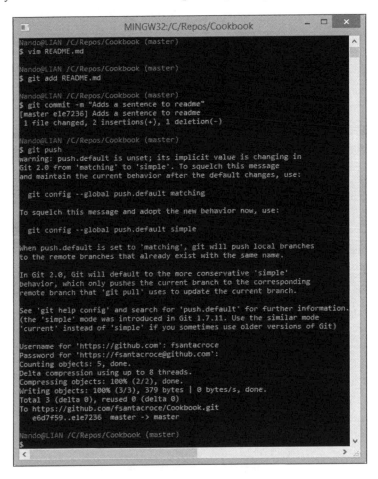

The `git push` command allows you to upload local work to a configured remote location, in this case, a remote GitHub repository. There are a few things we have to know about pushing. We can begin to understand the message Git gave us just after we run the `git push` command.

What do I send to the remote when I push?

When you give the `git push` command without specifying anything else, Git sends to the remote all the new commits you did locally in your actual branch. For new commits, we will send only the local commits that have not been uploaded yet.

The messages that appeared earlier tell us that something is about to change in the default behavior of the `git push` command. Before the incoming Git 2.0 release, when you fire the push command without specifying anything else, the default behavior is to push all the new commits in all the corresponding local-remote branches.

In this brand new `Cookbook` repository, we only have the `master` branch. However, next, you will learn how to deal with the remote having many branches.

Pushing a new branch to the remote

Obviously, we can create and push a new branch to the remote to make our work public and visible to other collaborators. For instance, I will create a new branch for my first recipe; then, I will push this branch to the remote GitHub server. Follow these simple steps:

1. Create a new branch, for instance, `Pasta`: `git checkout -b Pasta`.
2. Add to it a new file, for example, `Spaghetti-Carbonara.md`, and commit it.
3. Push the branch to the remote using `git push -u origin Pasta`.

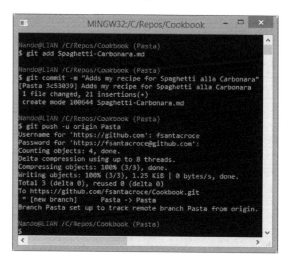

Before continuing, we have to examine in depth some things that happened after we used the `git push` command.

The origin

With the `git push -u origin Pasta` command, we told Git to upload our `Pasta` branch (and the commits within it) to the origin. The origin is the default remote name of a repository, like `master` is the default branch name. When you clone a repository from a remote, that remote becomes your `origin` alias. When you tell Git to push or pull something, you often have to tell it about the remote you want to use. Using the `origin` alias, you tell Git that you want to use your default remote.

If you want to see remotes actually configured in your repository, you could type a simple `git remote` command, followed by `-v` (`--verbose`) to get some more details:

In the details, you will see the full URL of the remote.

You can add, update, and delete remotes using the `git remote` command. We will make use of it when we need to. For now, just remember that there is a command for that.

Tracking branches

Using the `-u` option, we told Git to track the remote branch. Tracking a remote branch is the way to tie your local branch with the remote one. Note that this behavior is not automatic; you have to set it if you want it (Git does nothing until you ask for it!). When a local branch tracks a remote branch, you actually have a local and remote branch that can be kept easily in sync. This is very useful when you have to collaborate with some remote coworkers at the same branch, allowing all of them to keep their work in sync with other people's changes.

Furthermore, consider that when you use the `git fetch` command, you will get changes from all tracked branches. While you use the `git push` command, the default behavior is to push to the corresponding remote branch only.

To better understand the way our repository is now configured, try to type `git remote show origin`:

```
MINGW32:/C/Repos/Cookbook                          —  □  ×

Nando@LIAN /C/Repos/Cookbook (Pasta)
$ git remote show origin
* remote origin
  Fetch URL: https://github.com/fsantacroce/Cookbook.git
  Push  URL: https://github.com/fsantacroce/Cookbook.git
  HEAD branch: master
  Remote branches:
    Pasta  tracked
    master tracked
  Local branches configured for 'git pull':
    Pasta  merges with remote Pasta
    master merges with remote master
  Local refs configured for 'git push':
    Pasta  pushes to Pasta  (up to date)
    master pushes to master (up to date)

Nando@LIAN /C/Repos/Cookbook (Pasta)
$
```

As you can see, both the `Pasta` and `master` branches are tracked.

You can also see that your local branches are configured to push and pull to remote branches with the same name. However, remember that it is not mandatory to have local and remote branches with the same name. The local branch `foo` can track the remote branch `bar` and vice versa; there are no restrictions.

Downloading remote changes

The first thing you have to learn when working with remote branches is to check whether there are modifications to retrieve.

Checking for modifications and downloading them

The `git fetch` command is very helpful. To see it at work, create a new file directly on GitHub using the following steps so that we can work with it:

1. Go to your GitHub dashboard and choose the `Pasta` branch.

2. Click the plus icon on the right-hand side of the repository name to add a new file.

3. Add a new empty file, for example, `Bucatini-Amatriciana.md`, and commit it directly from GitHub:

Now, we can make use of `git fetch`:

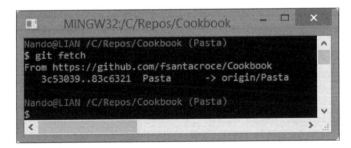

The `git fetch` command downloads differences from the remote, but does not apply them. With the help of `git status`, we will see more details:

As you can see, Git tells us there is one downloaded commit we have to apply to keep our branch in sync with the remote counterpart.

Applying downloaded changes

If **push** is the verb used to define the upload part of the work, **pull** is the verb used to describe the action of downloading and applying remote changes. When you pull something from a remote, Git will retrieve all the remote commits made after your last pull from the branch you specify and merge them. Of course, the local destination branch is the branch you are in now (if you don't explicitly specify another one). So, finally, the pull command is the `git fetch` command plus the `git merge` command (in the future, you can skip `git fetch` and use only `git pull` to merge remote commits).

Now, use the `git pull` command to merge the brand new `Bucatini-Amatriciana.md` file committed directly from GitHub:

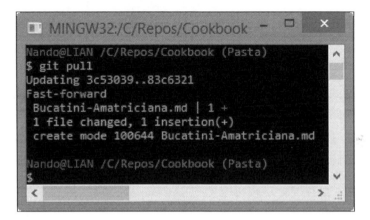

Well done! Now, our `Pasta` branch is in sync with the remote one. We have the `Bucatini-Amatriciana.md` file in our local branch, ready to be filled.

Just to end this simple example, make some modifications to the new downloaded file and push the commit to GitHub:

```
MINGW32:/C/Repos/Cookbook                                    —  □   ×

Nando@LIAN /C/Repos/Cookbook (Pasta)
$ git add Bucatini-Amatriciana.md

Nando@LIAN /C/Repos/Cookbook (Pasta)
$ git commit -m "Adds ingredients for Bucatini all'Amatriciana recipe"
[Pasta 4af2045] Adds ingredients for Bucatini all'Amatriciana recipe
 1 file changed, 15 insertions(+)

Nando@LIAN /C/Repos/Cookbook (Pasta)
$ git push origin Pasta
Username for 'https://github.com': fsantacroce
Password for 'https://fsantacroce@github.com':
Counting objects: 6, done.
Delta compression using up to 8 threads.
Compressing objects: 100% (3/3), done.
Writing objects: 100% (3/3), 790 bytes | 0 bytes/s, done.
Total 3 (delta 0), reused 0 (delta 0)
To https://github.com/fsantacroce/Cookbook.git
   83c6321..4af2045  Pasta -> Pasta

Nando@LIAN /C/Repos/Cookbook (Pasta)
$
```

This time we have specified the branch where we want to push changes, so Git avoids reminding us the default `git push` behavior is going to change in the next release.

Going backward: publish a local repository to GitHub

Often, you will find yourself needing to put your local repository in a shared place where someone else can look at your work. In this section, we will learn how to achieve this.

Create a new local repository to publish by following these simple steps:

1. Go to our C:\Repos folder.

2. Create a new HelloWorld folder.

3. Init a new repository, as we did in *Chapter 1, Getting Started with Git.*

4. Add a new README.md file and commit it.

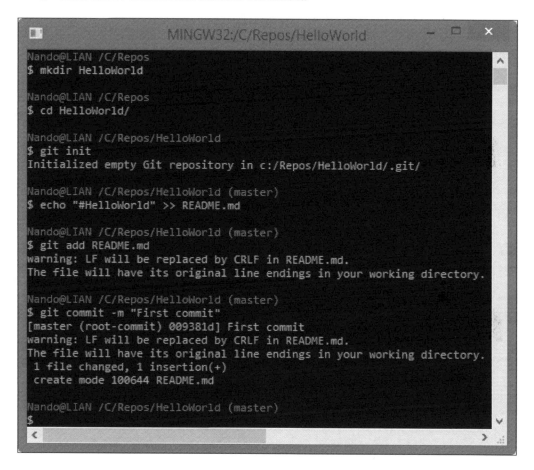

Now, create the GitHub repository as we did previously. This time, leave it empty. Don't initialize it with a README.md file; we already have one in our local repository:

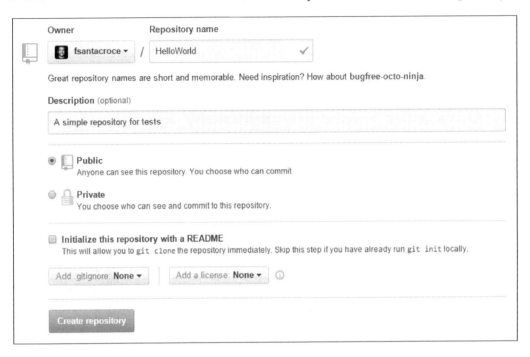

At this point, we are ready to publish our local repository on GitHub or, more specifically, add a remote to it.

Adding a remote to a local repository

To publish our HelloWorld repository, we simply have to add its first remote. Adding a remote is quite simple: Use the command git remote add origin <remote-repository-url>.

So, type git remote add origin https://github.com/fsantacroce/HelloWorld.git in the Bash shell.

Adding a remote, like adding or modifying other configuration parameters, simply consists of editing some text files in the .git folder. In the next chapter, we will take a look at some of these files.

Pushing a local branch to a remote repository

After adding a remote, push your local changes to the remote using `git push -u origin master`:

```
Nando@LIAN /C/Repos/HelloWorld (master)
$ git remote add origin https://github.com/fsantacroce/HelloWorld.git

Nando@LIAN /C/Repos/HelloWorld (master)
$ git push -u origin master
Username for 'https://github.com': fsantacroce
Password for 'https://fsantacroce@github.com':
Counting objects: 3, done.
Writing objects: 100% (3/3), 231 bytes | 0 bytes/s, done.
Total 3 (delta 0), reused 0 (delta 0)
To https://github.com/fsantacroce/HelloWorld.git
 * [new branch]      master -> master
Branch master set up to track remote branch master from origin.

Nando@LIAN /C/Repos/HelloWorld (master)
$
```

That's all!

Social coding – collaborate using GitHub

GitHub's trademark is the so-called **social coding**. Right from the beginning, GitHub made it easy to share code, track other people's work, and collaborate using two basic concepts: forks and pull requests. In this section, I will illustrate these concepts in brief.

Forking a repository

Forking is a common concept for a developer. If you have already used a GNU-Linux-based distribution, you would know that there are some forefathers, such as Debian, and some derived distro, such as Ubuntu. They are commonly called the **forks** of the original distribution.

In GitHub, things are similar. At some point, you will find an interesting open-source project that you want to modify slightly to perfectly fit your needs. At the same time, you want to benefit from bug fixes and new features from the original project, all the time keeping in touch with your work. The right thing to do in this situation is to fork the project.

However, first, remember that fork is not a Git feature, but a GitHub invention. When you fork on GitHub, you get a server-side clone of the repository on your GitHub account. If you clone your forked repository locally in the remote list, you would find the `origin` alias that points to your account repository. The original repository will generally assume the `upstream` alias (but this is not automatic, you have to add it manually):

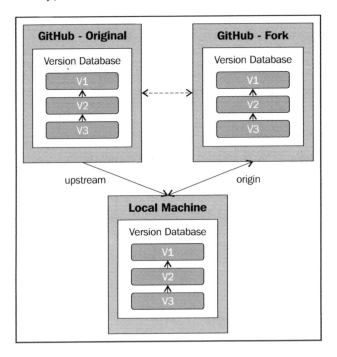

For your convenience, the right command to add the `upstream` remote is `$ git remote add upstream https://github.com/<original-owner>/<original-repository>.git`.

Now, to better understand this feature, go to your GitHub account and try to fork a common GitHub repository called `Spoon-Knife`, made by the `octocat` GitHub mascot user. Perform the following steps:

1. Log in to your GitHub account.

2. Look for `spoon-knife` using the search textbox located in the top-left corner of the page:

3. Click on the first result, `octocat/Spoon-Knife` repository.

4. Fork the repository using the **Fork** button at the right of the page:

5. After a funny photocopy animation, you will get a brand new `Spoon-Knife` repository on your GitHub account:

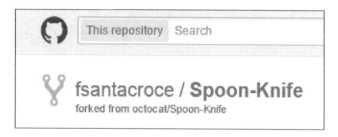

Now, you can clone this repository locally, as we did earlier:

```
Nando@LIAN /C/Repos
$ git clone https://github.com/fsantacroce/Spoon-Knife.git
Cloning into 'Spoon-Knife'...
remote: Counting objects: 16, done.
remote: Total 16 (delta 0), reused 0 (delta 0)
Unpacking objects: 100% (16/16), done.
Checking connectivity... done.

Nando@LIAN /C/Repos
$ cd Spoon-Knife/

Nando@LIAN /C/Repos/Spoon-Knife (master)
$ git remote -v
origin  https://github.com/fsantacroce/Spoon-Knife.git (fetch)
origin  https://github.com/fsantacroce/Spoon-Knife.git (push)

Nando@LIAN /C/Repos/Spoon-Knife (master)
$
```

As you can see, the `upstream` remote is not present. This is a convention, not a thing that belongs to Git itself. To add this remote, type:

```
git remote add upstream https://github.com/octocat/Spoon-Knife.git
```

Now, you can keep your local repository in sync with the changes in your remote and the `origin` alias. You can also get changes ones coming from the `upstream` remote, the original repository you forked. At this point, you are probably wondering how to deal with two different remotes. Well, it is easy. Simply pull from `upstream` and merge those modifications in your local repository. Then, push them in your `origin` remote in addition to your changes. If someone else clones your repository, they would receive your work merged with the work done by someone else on the original repository.

Submitting pull requests

If you created a fork of a repository, this is because you are not a direct contributor of the original project or simply because you don't want to make a mess in other people's work before you are familiar with the code.

However, at a certain point, you realize that your work can be useful even for the original project. You realize that you can implement a previous piece of code in a better way, you can add a missing feature, and so on.

So, you find yourself needing to allow the original author to know you did something interesting, to ask them if they want to take a look and, maybe, integrate your work. This is the moment when pull requests come in handy.

A pull request is a way to tell the original author, "Hey! I did something interesting using your original code. Do you want to take a look and integrate my work, if you find it good enough?" This is not only a technical way to achieve the purpose of integrating work, but it is even a powerful practice to promote **code reviews** (and then the so-called social coding) as recommended by the eXtreme Programming fellows (http://en.wikipedia.org/wiki/Extreme_programming).

One other reason to use a pull request is because you cannot push directly to the `upstream` remote if you are not a contributor of the original project. Pull requests are the only way. In small scenarios (such as a team of two or three developers that works in the same room), probably, the `fork` and `pull` model represents an overhead. So, it is more common to directly share the original repository with all the contributors, skipping the fork and pull ceremony.

Creating a pull request

To create a pull request, you have to go to your GitHub account and make it directly from your forked account. However, first, you have to know that pull requests can be made only from separated branches. At this point of the book, you are probably used to creating a new branch for a new feature or refactor purpose. So, this is nothing new.

To try, let's create a local `TeaSpoon` branch in our repository, commit a new file, and push it to our GitHub account:

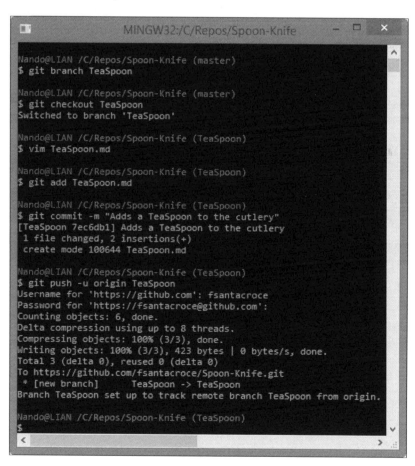

If you take a look at your account, you will find a surprise: in your `Spoon-Knife` repository, there is now a new green button made on purpose to start a pull request:

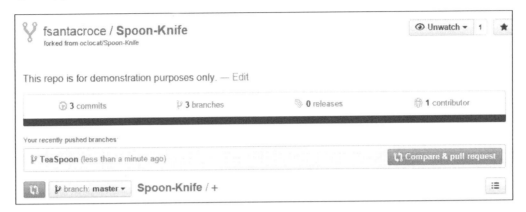

Clicking on this button makes GitHub open a new page where we can adorn our pull request to better support our work. We can let the original author know why we think our work can be useful even in the original project.

However, let me analyze this new page in brief.

In the top-left corner, you will find what branches GitHub is about to compare for you:

This means that you are about to compare your local `TeaSpoon` branch with the original `master` branch of the `octocat` user. At the bottom of the page, you can see all the different details (files added, removed, changed, and so on):

In the central part of the page, you can describe the work you did in your branch. After that, you have to click on the green **Create pull request** button to send your request to the original author, allowing him to access your work and analyze it. A green **Able to merge** sticker on the right-hand side informs you that these two branches can be automatically merged (there are no unresolved conflicts, which is always good to see, considering your work):

Now, the last step: click on the **Create pull request** button and cross your fingers.

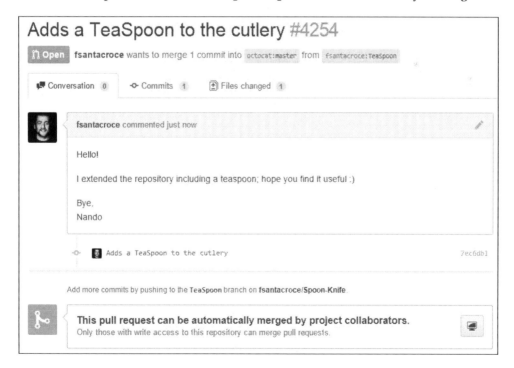

At this point a new conversation begins. You and the project collaborators can start to discuss your work. During this period, you and other collaborators can change the code to better fit common needs, until an original repository collaborator decides to accept your request or discard it, thus closing the pull request.

Summary

In this chapter, we finally got in touch with the Git ability to manage multiple remote copies of repositories. This gives you a wide range of possibilities to better organize your collaboration workflow inside your team.

In the next chapter, you will learn some advanced techniques using well-known and niche commands. This will make you a more secure and proficient Git user, allowing you to easily resolve some common issues that occur in a developer's life.

4
Git Fundamentals – Niche Concepts, Configurations, and Commands

This chapter is a collection of short but useful tricks to make our Git experience more comfortable. In the first three chapters, we learnt all the concepts we need to take the first steps into versioning systems using the Git tool; now it's time to go a little bit more in depth to discover some other powerful weapons in the Git arsenal and see how to use them (without shooting yourself in your foot, preferably).

Dissecting the Git configuration

In the first part of this chapter, we will learn how to enhance our Git configuration to better fit our needs and speed up the daily work; now it's time to become familiar with the configuration internals.

Configuration architecture

The configuration options are stored in plain text files. The `git config` command is just a convenient tool to edit these files without the hassle of remembering where they are stored and opening them in a text editor.

Configuration levels

In Git we have three configuration levels which are:

- System
- User
- Repository

There are different configuration files for every different configuration level.

You can basically set every parameter at every level according to your needs. If you set the same parameters at different levels, the lowest-level parameter hides the top level parameters; so, for example, if you set user.name at global level, it will hide the one eventually set up at system level; if you set it at repository level, it will hide the one specified at global level and the one eventually set up at system level.

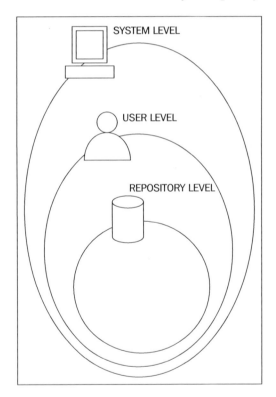

System level

The system level contains **system-wide configurations**; if you edit the configuration at this level, every user and its repository will be affected.

This configuration is stored in the `gitconfig` file usually located in:

- Windows - `C:\Program Files (x86)\Git\etc\gitconfig`
- Linux - `/etc/gitconfig`
- Mac OS X - `/usr/local/git/etc/gitconfig`

To edit the parameters at this level, you have to use the `--system` option; please note that it requires administrative privileges (for example, root permission on Linux and Mac OS X). Anyway, as a rule of thumb, the edit configuration at system level is discouraged in favor of per user configuration modification.

Global level

The global level contains **user-wide configurations**; if you edit the configuration at this level, every user's repository will be affected.

This configuration is stored in the `.gitconfig` file usually located in:

- Windows - `C:\Users\<UserName>\.gitconfig`
- Linux - `~/.gitconfig`
- Mac OS X - `~/.gitconfig`

To edit the parameters at this level, you have to use the `--global` option.

Repository level

The repository level contains **repository only configurations**; if you edit the configuration at this level, only the repository in use will be affected.

This configuration is stored in the `config` file located in the `.git` repository subfolder:

- Windows - `C:\<MyRepoFolder>\.git\config`
- Linux - `~/<MyRepoFolder>/.git/config`
- Mac OS X - `~/<MyRepoFolder>/.git/config`

To edit parameters at this level, you can use the `--local` option or simply avoid using any option as this is the default one.

Listing configurations

To get a list of all configurations currently in use, you can run the `git config` `--list` option; if you are inside a repository, it will show all the configurations from repository to system level. To filter the list, append `--system`, `--global`, or `--local` options to obtain only the desired level configurations, as shown in the following screenshot:

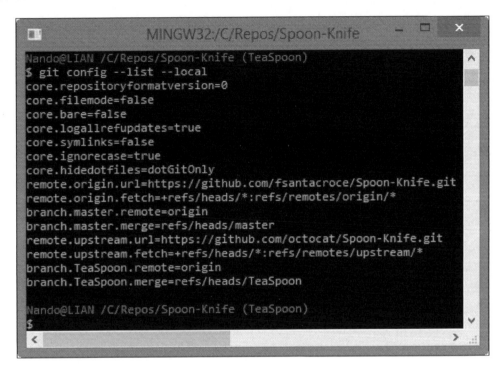

Editing configuration files manually

Even if it is generally discouraged, you can modify Git configurations by directly editing the files. Git configuration files are quite easy to understand, so when you look on the Internet for a particular configuration you want to set, it is not unusual to find just the right corresponding text lines; the only little foresight to maintain in those cases is that you always need to back up files before editing them. In the next paragraphs, we will try to make some changes in this manner.

Setting up other environment configurations

Using Git can be a painful experience if you are not able to place it conveniently inside your work environment. Let's start to shape some rough edges using a bunch of custom configurations.

Basic configurations

In the previous chapters, we saw that we can change a Git variable value using the `git config` command with the `<variable.name>` `<value>` syntax. In this paragraph, we will make use of the `config` command to vary some Git behaviors.

Typos autocorrection

So, let's try to fix an annoying question about the typing command named **typos**. I often find myself re-typing the same command two or more times; Git can help us with embedded **autocorrection**, but we first have to enable it. To enable it, you have to modify the `help.autocorrection` parameter, defining how many tenths of a second Git will wait before running the assumed command; so by giving a `help.autocorrect 10` command, Git will wait for a second, as shown in the following screenshot:

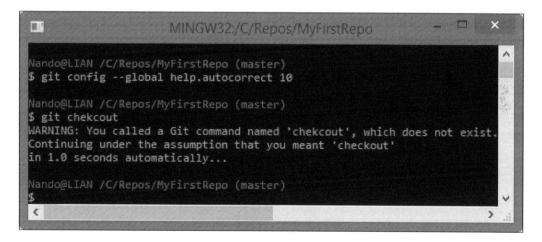

To abort the autocorrection, simply type *Ctrl + C*.

Now that you know about configuration files, you can note that the parameters we set by the command line are in this form: `section.parameter_name`. You can see the sections' names within `[]` if you look in the configuration file; for example, you can find them in `C:\Users\<UserName>\.gitconfig`, as shown in the following screenshot:

```
39          trustExitCode = true
40
41    [help]
42          autocorrect = 10
43    [push]
44          default = tracking
45

Normal text file                    length : 12
```

Push default

We already talked about the `git push` command and its default behavior. To avoid such annoying issues, it is a good practice to set a more convenient default behavior for this command.

There are two ways we can do this. The first one is to set Git to ask to us the name of the branch we want to push every time, so a simple `git push` will have no effects. To obtain this, set `push.default` to `nothing`, as shown in the following screenshot:

```
                    MINGW32:/C/Repos/Cookbook                    — □ ✕

Nando@LIAN /C/Repos/Cookbook (Pasta)
$ git config --global push.default nothing

Nando@LIAN /C/Repos/Cookbook (Pasta)
$ git push
fatal: You didn't specify any refspecs to push, and push.default is "nothing".

Nando@LIAN /C/Repos/Cookbook (Pasta)
$
```

As you can see, now Git pretends that you specify the target branch at every push.

This may be too restrictive, but at least you can avoid common mistakes like pushing some personal local branches to the remote, generating confusion in the team.

Another way to save yourself from this kind of mistake is to set the `push.default` parameter to `simple`, allowing Git to push only when there is a remote branch with the same name as that of the local one, as shown in the following screenshot:

This action will push the local tracked branch to the remote.

Defining the default editor

Some people really don't like `vim`, even only for writing commit messages; if you are one of those people, there is good news for you in that you can change it instead by setting the `core.default` config parameter:

```
$ git config --global core.editor notepad
```

Obviously you can set all text editors on the market. If you are a Windows user, remember that the full path of the editor has to be in the PATH environment variable; basically, if you can run your preferred editor typing its executable name in a DOS shell, you can use it even in a Bash shell with Git.

Other configurations

You can browse a wide list of other configuration variables at http://git-scm.com/docs/git-config.

Git aliases

In *Chapter 2*, *Git Fundamentals – Working Locally* we already mentioned Git aliases and their purpose; in this paragraph, I will suggest only a few more to help you make things easier.

Shortcuts to common commands

One thing you can find useful is to shorten common commands like `git checkout` and so on; therefore, these are some useful aliases:

```
$ git config --global alias.co checkout
```

```
$ git config --global alias.br branch
```

```
$ git config --global alias.ci commit
```

```
$ git config --global alias.st status
```

Another common practice is to shorten a command by adding one or more options that you use all the time; for example set a `git cm <commit message>` command shortcut to alias `git commit -m <commit message>`:

```
$ git config --global alias.cm "commit -m"
```

Creating commands

Another common way to customize the Git experience is to create commands you think should exist, as we did in *Chapter 2*, *Git Fundamentals – Working Locally* with the `git tree` command.

git unstage

The classic example is the `git unstage` alias:

```
$ git config --global alias.unstage 'reset HEAD --'
```

With this alias, you can remove a file from the index in a more meaningful way as compared to the equivalent `git reset HEAD <file>` syntax:

```
$ git unstage myfile.txt
$ git reset HEAD myfile.txt
```

git undo

Do you want a fast way to revert the last ongoing commit? Create a `git undo` alias:

```
$ git config --global alias.undo 'reset --soft HEAD~1'
```

You will be tempted to use the `--hard` option instead of the `--soft` option, but simply don't do it as it's generally a bad idea to make it too easy to destroy information, and sooner or later, you will regret for deleting something important.

git last

A `git last` alias is useful to read about your last commit, which is shown here:

```
$ git config --global alias.last 'log -1 HEAD'
```

```
MINGW32:/C/Repos/MyFirstRepo

Nando@LIAN /C/Repos/MyFirstRepo (master)
$ git config --global alias.last 'log -1 HEAD'

Nando@LIAN /C/Repos/MyFirstRepo (master)
$ git last
commit abd8be1ef75eec7ed4554dae3508287d0d843796
Author: Ferdinando Santacroce <ferdinando.santacroce@gmail.com>
Date:    Thu Jan 1 17:23:52 2015 +0100

    My commit message

Nando@LIAN /C/Repos/MyFirstRepo (master)
$
```

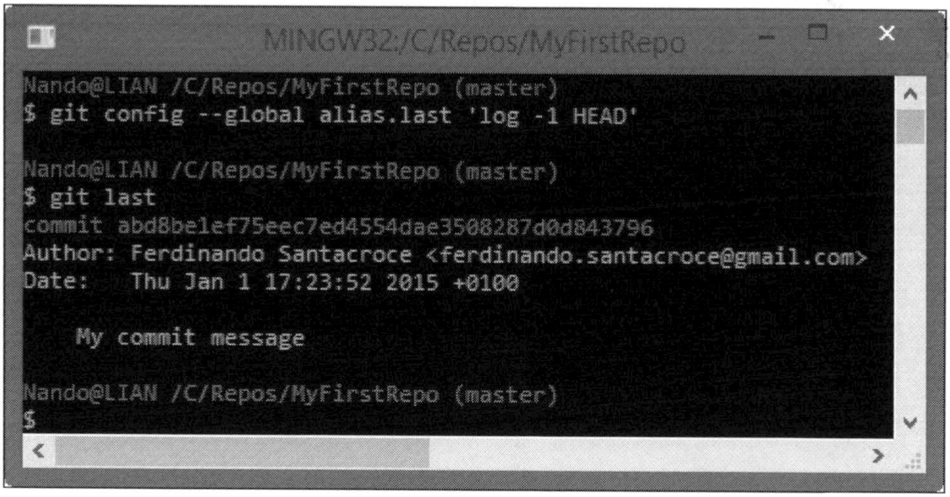

git difflast

With `git difflast` alias, you can indeed see a difference from your last commit, as shown here:

```
$ git config --global alias.difflast 'diff --cached HEAD^'
```

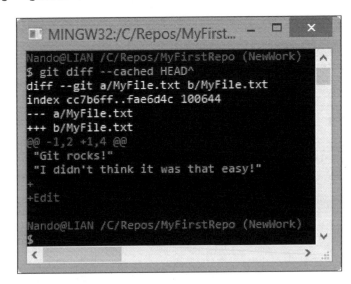

Advanced aliases with external commands

If you want the alias to run external shell commands instead of a Git subcommand, you have to prefix the alias with a `!`:

```
$ git config --global alias.echo !echo
```

Suppose you are annoyed by the canonical `git add <file>` plus `git commit <file>` sequence of commands, and you want to do it in a single shot; here you can call the `git` command twice in sequence creating this alias:

```
$ git config --global alias.cm '!git add -A && git commit -m'
```

With this alias you commit all the files, adding them before, if necessary.

Have you noted that I set again the `cm` alias? If you set an already configured alias, the previous alias will be overwritten.

There are also aliases that define and use complex functions or scripts, but I'll leave it to the curiosity of the reader to explore these aliases. If you are looking for inspiration, please take a look at mine at `https://github.com/jesuswasrasta/GitEnvironment`.

Removing an alias

Removing an alias is quite easy; you have to use the `--unset` option, specifying the alias to remove. For example, if you want to remove the `cm` alias, you have to run:

```
$ git config --global --unset alias.cm
```

Note that you have to specify the configuration level with the appropriate option; in this case, we are removing the alias from the user (`--global`) level.

Aliasing the git command itself

I already said I'm a bad typewriter; if you are too, you can alias the git command itself (using the default `alias` command in Bash):

```
$ alias gti='git'
```

In this manner, you will save some other keyboard strokes. Note that this is not a Git alias but a Bash shell alias.

Git references

We said that a Git repository can be imagined as an acyclic graph, where every node, the commit, has a parent and a unique SHA-1 identifier. But during the previous chapters, we even used some references such as the HEAD, branches, tags, and so on.

Git manages these references as files in the `.git/refs` repository folder:

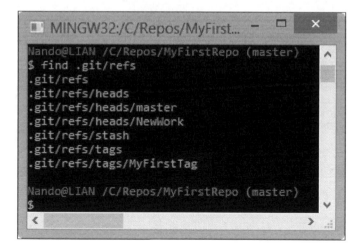

If you open one of those files, you will find it inside the SHA-1 of the commit they are tied to. As you can see, there are subfolders for tags and branches (called `heads`).

Symbolic references

The `HEAD` file instead is located in the `.git` folder, as shown in the following screenshot:

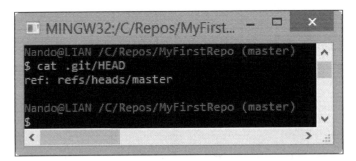

`HEAD` is a **symbolic reference**; symbolic references are references that point to other references, using the `ref: <reference>` syntax. In this case, the `HEAD` is currently pointing to the `master` branch; if you check out another branch, you will see the file's content change, as shown in the following screenshot:

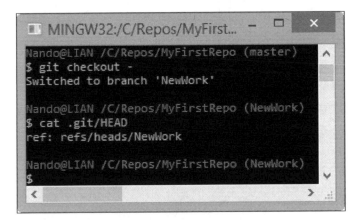

Ancestry references

In Git you often need to reference the past (for example, the last commit); for this scope, we can use two different special characters which are the **tilde** ~ and the **caret** ^.

The first parent

Suppose you want to completely delete the last **x4y5z6** commit:

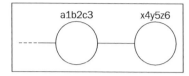

A way to do this is to move the HEAD pointer to the **a1b2c3** commit, using the --hard option:

```
$ git reset --hard a1b2c3
```

Another way to do this is to move the pointer back to the parent commit. To define the parent, you have to specify a starting point reference, which can be the HEAD, a specific commit, a tag, or a branch and then one of two special characters: the tilde ~, for the first parent and the caret ^ for the second one (remember that commits can have two parents when they represent a merge result).

Let's get under the lens of the tilde ~. With the <ref>~<number> notation, we can specify how many steps backward we are going to take; going back to the example, an equivalent of the previous command is this:

```
$ git reset --hard HEAD~1
```

The HEAD~1 notation tells Git to point to the first parent commit of the actual commit (the HEAD, indeed). Note that HEAD~1 and HEAD~ are equivalent.

You can also go backward by more than one step, simply incrementing the number; a HEAD~3 reference will point to the third ancestor of the HEAD:

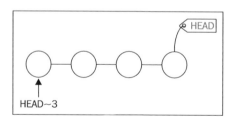

The second parent

With the ^ caret character, instead we reference the second parent of a commit, but only starting from the number **2**; the ref^1 notation references the first parent, as does the ref~1 notation whereas ref^ and ref~1 are equivalent. Also note that ref^1 and ref^ are equivalent.

The ^ and ~ operators can be combined; here's a diagram showing how to reference various commits using HEAD as the starting point:

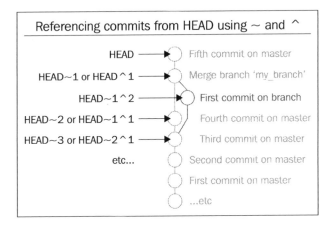

World-wide techniques

In this section, you will raise your skills by learning some techniques that will come in handy in different situations.

Changing the last commit message

This trick is for people who don't double-check what they're writing. If you pressed the *Enter* key too early, there's a way to modify the last commit message, using the git commit command with the --amend option:

```
$ git commit --amend -m "New commit message"
```

Please note that with the --amend option, you are actually redoing the commit, which will have a new hash; if you already pushed the previous commit, changing the last commit is not recommended; rather, it is deplorable and you will get in trouble.

Tracing changes in a file

Working on source code in a team, it is not uncommon to need to look at the last modifications made to a particular file to better understand how it evolved over time. To achieve this result, we can use the git blame <filename> command.

Let's try this inside the `Spoon-Knife` repository to see the changes made to the `README.md` file during that time:

As you can see in the preceding screenshot, the result reports all the affected lines of the `README.md` file; for every line you can see the commit hash, the author, the date, and the row number of the text file lines.

Suppose now you found that the modification you are looking for is the one made in the **d0dd1f61** commit; to see what happened there, type the `git show` `d0dd1f61` command:

The `git show` command is a multipurpose command, it can show you one or more objects; in this case we have used it to show the modification made in a particular commit using the `git show <commit-hash>` format.

The `git blame` and `git show` commands have quite a long list of options; the purpose of this paragraph is only to point the reader to the way changes should be traced on a file; you can inspect other possibilities using the ever useful `git <command> --help` command.

The last tip I want to suggest is to use the Git GUI:

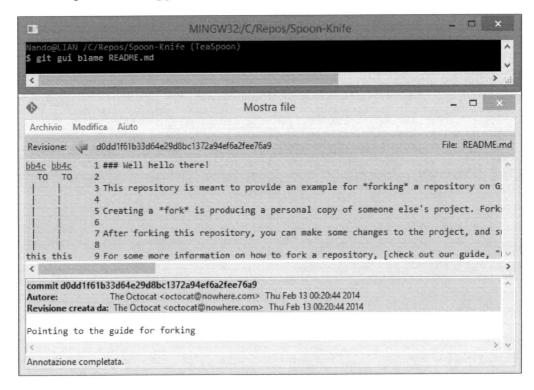

With the help of GUI, things are much more easy to understand.

Cherry picking

The **cherry picking** activity consists of choosing existing commits from somewhere else and applying them here. I will make use of an example to better explain how you can benefit from this technique.

Suppose you and your colleague Mark are working on two different public branches of the same repository; Mark found and fixed an annoying bug in the feat1 branch that affects even your feat2 branch. You need that fix, but you can't (or don't want to) merge his branch, so how can you benefit from his fix?

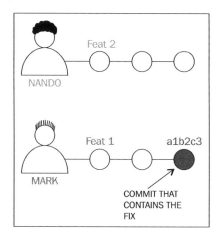

It's easy; get the commit that fixes that bug and apply it to your current branch, using the `git cherry-pick` command:

```
$ git checkout feat2
$ git cherry-pick a1b2c3
```

That's all! Now the commit **a1b2c3** performed by Mark in the `feat1` branch has been applied to the `feat2` branch and committed as a new **x4y5z6** commit, as shown in the following screenshot:

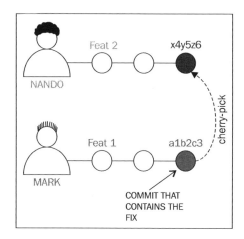

The `git cherry-pick` command behaves just like the `git merge` command. If Git can't apply the changes (for example, you get merge conflicts), it leaves you to resolve the conflicts manually and make the commit yourself.

We can even pick commit sets if we want to by using the `<starting-commit>..<ending-commit>` syntax:

```
$ git cherry-pick feat1~2..feat1~0
```

With this syntax, you are basically picking the last two commits from the `feat1` branch.

Tricks

In this section, I would suggest just a bunch of tips and tricks that I found useful in the past.

Bare repositories

Bare repositories are repositories that do not contain working copy files but contain only the `.git` folder. A bare repository is essentially for sharing; if you use Git in a centralized way, pushing and pulling to a common remote (a local server, a GitHub repository, or so on), you will agree that the remote has no interest in checking out files you work on; the scope of that remote is only to be a central point of contact for the team, so having working copy files in it is a waste of space, and no one will edit them directly on the remote.

If you want to set up a bare repository, you have to use only the `--bare` option:

```
$ git init --bare NewRepository.git
```

As you may have noticed, I called it `NewRepository.git`, using a `.git` extension; this is not mandatory but is a common way to identify bare repositories. If you pay attention, you will note that even in GitHub every repository ends with the `.git` extension.

Converting a regular repository to a bare one

It can happen that you start working on a project in a local repository and then you feel the need to move it to a centralized server to make it available to other people or locations.

You can easily convert a regular repository to a bare one using the `git clone` command with the same `--bare` option:

```
$ git clone --bare my_project my_project.git
```

In this manner, you have a 1:1 copy of your repository, but in a bare version, ready to be shared.

Backup repositories

If you need a backup, there are two commands you can use, one of which is for archiving only files and the other is for backing up the entire bundle including the versioning information.

Archiving the repository

To archive the repository without including the versioning information, you can use the `git archive` command; there are many output formats of which ZIP is the classic one:

```
$ git archive master --format=zip --output=../repbck.zip
```

Please note that using this command is not the same as backing up folders in the filesystem; as you noticed, the `git archive` command can produce archives in a smarter way, including only files in a branch or even in a single commit. By doing this, you are archiving only the last commit, as shown in the following code:

```
$ git archive HEAD --format=zip --output=../headbck.zip
```

Archiving files in this way can be useful if you have to share your code with people that don't have Git installed.

Bundling the repository

Another interesting command is the `git bundle` command. With `git bundle` you can export a snapshot from your repository, and you can then restore it.

Suppose you want to clone your repository on another computer, and the network is down or absent; with this command, you create a `repo.bundle` file of the `master` branch:

```
$ git bundle create ../repo.bundle master
```

With these other commands, we can then restore the bundle in the other computer using the `git clone` command, as shown here:

```
$ cd /OtherComputer/Folder
$ git clone repo.bundle repo -b master
```

Summary

In this chapter, you enhanced your knowledge about Git and its wide set of commands. You finally understood how configuration levels work and how to set your preferences using Git, by adding useful command aliases to the shell. Then we looked at how Git deals with references, providing a way to refer to a previous commit using its degree of relationship.

Furthermore, you added some key techniques to your skill set, as it is important to learn something you will use as soon as you start to use Git extensively. You also learned some simple tricks to help you use Git more efficiently.

5
Obtaining the Most – Good Commits and Workflows

Now that we are familiar with Git and versioning systems, it's time to look at the whole thing from a much higher perspective to become aware of common patterns and procedures.

In this chapter, we will walk through some of the most common ways to organize and build meaningful commits and repositories. We will obtain not only a well-organized code stack, but also a meaningful source of information.

The art of committing

While working with Git, committing seems the easiest part of the job: you add files, write a short comment, and then, you're done. However, it is because of its simplicity that often, especially at the very beginning of your experience, you acquire the bad habit of doing terrible commits: too late, too big, too short, or simply equipped with bad messages.

Now, we will take some time to identify possible issues, drawing attention to tips and hints to get rid of these bad habits.

Building the right commit

One of the harder skills to acquire while programming in general is to split the work in small and meaningful tasks.

Too often, I have experienced this scenario. You start to fix a small issue in a file. Then, you see another piece of code that can be easily improved, even if it is not related to what you are working on now. You can't resist it, and you fix it. At the end and after a small time, you find yourself with tons of *concurrent* files and *changes* to commit.

At this point, things get worse, because usually, programmers are lazy people. So, they don't write all the important things to describe changes in the commit message. In commit messages, you start to write sentences such as "Some fixes to this and that", "Removed old stuff", "Tweaks", and so on, without anything that helps other programmers understand what you have done.

COMMENT	DATE
CREATED MAIN LOOP & TIMING CONTROL	14 HOURS AGO
ENABLED CONFIG FILE PARSING	9 HOURS AGO
MISC BUGFIXES	5 HOURS AGO
CODE ADDITIONS/EDITS	4 HOURS AGO
MORE CODE	4 HOURS AGO
HERE HAVE CODE	4 HOURS AGO
AAAAAAAA	3 HOURS AGO
ADKFJSLKDFJSDKLFJ	3 HOURS AGO
MY HANDS ARE TYPING WORDS	2 HOURS AGO
HAAAAAAAANDS	2 HOURS AGO

AS A PROJECT DRAGS ON, MY GIT COMMIT MESSAGES GET LESS AND LESS INFORMATIVE.

Courtesy of http://xkcd.com/1296/

At the end, you realize that your repository is only a dump where you empty your index now and then. I have seen some people committing only at the end of the day (and not every day) to keep a backup of the data or because someone else needed the changes reflected on their computer.

Another side effect is that the resulting repository history becomes useless for anything other than retrieving content at a given point in time.

The following tips can help you turn your **Version Control System** (**VCS**) from a backup system into a valuable tool for communication and documentation.

Make only one change per commit

After the routine morning coffee, you open your editor and start to work on a bug, BUG42. While working around fixing the bug in the code, you realize that fixing BUG79 will require tweaking just a single line of code. So, you fix it. However, you not only change that awful class name, but also add a good-looking label to the form and make a few more changes. The damage is done.

How can you wrap up all that work in a meaningful commit now? Maybe, in the meantime, you went home for lunch, talked to your boss about another project, and you can't even remember all the little things you did.

In this scenario, there is only one way to limit the damage: split the files to commit among more than one commit. Sometimes, this helps to reduce the pain, but it is only palliative. Very often, you modify the same file for different reasons, so doing this is quite difficult, if not impossible. The last hope is to use `git add -p` command, that let's you to stage only some modification on a file, grouping them in different commit to separate topics.

The only way to definitely solve this problem is to only make one change per commit. It seems easy, I know, but it is quite difficult to acquire this ability. There are no tools for this. No one, but you, can help. It only needs discipline, the most lacking virtue in creative people such as programmers.

There are some tips to pursue this aim; let's have a look at them together.

Split up features and tasks

As said earlier, breaking up the things to do is a fine art. If you know and adopt some **Agile movement** techniques, you will have probably faced these problems. So, you have an advantage; otherwise, you will need some more effort, but it is not something that you can't achieve.

Consider that you have been assigned to add the **Remember me** check in the login page of a web application, like the one shown here:

This feature is quite small, but implies changes at different levels. To accomplish this, you'll have to:

- Modify the UI to add the check control
- Pass the "is checked" information through different layers
- Store this information somewhere
- Retrieve this information when needed
- Invalidate (set it to false) following some kind of policy (after 15 days, after 10 logins, and so on)

Do you think you can do all these things in one shot? Yes? You are wrong! Even if you estimate a couple of hours for an ordinary task, remember that Murphy's law is in ambush. You will receive four calls, your boss will look for you for three different meetings, and your computer will go up in flames.

This is one of the first things to learn: break up every work into small tasks. It does not matter whether you use timeboxing techniques such as the **Pomodoro Technique**; small things are always easy to handle. I'm not talking about split hairs, but try to organize your tasks into things you can do in a defined amount of time, hopefully a bunch of half hours, not days.

So, take a pen and paper and write down all the tasks, as we did earlier with the login page example. Do you think you can do all those things in a small amount of time? Maybe yes, maybe not: some tasks are bigger than others. That's OK; this is not a scientific method. It's a matter of experience. Can you split a task and create two other meaningful tasks? Do it.

Are you unable to do it? No problem; don't try to split tasks if they lose meaning.

Write commit messages before starting to code

Now, you have a list of tasks to do; pick the first and… start to code? No! Take another piece of paper and describe every task's step with a sentence. Magically, you will realize that every sentence can be the message of a single commit, where you describe the features you deleted, added, or changed in your software.

This kind of prior preparation helps you define modifications to implement (letting better software design to emerge). It also focuses on what is important and lowers down the stress of thinking at the versioning part of the work during the coding session. While you are facing a programming problem, your brain floods with little implementation details related to the code you are working on. So, the fewer the distractions, the better.

This is one of the best versioning-related hints I ever received. If you have just a quarter of an hour to spare, I recommend that you read the *Preemptive commit comments* blog post (`https://arialdomartini.wordpress.com/2012/09/03/pre-emptive-commit-comments/`) by *Arialdo Martini*. This is where I learnt this trick.

Include the whole change in one commit

Making more than one change per commit is a bad thing. However, splitting a single change into more than one commit is also considered harmful. As you may know, in some trained teams, you do not simply push your code to production. Before that, you have to pass some code quality reviews, where someone else tries to understand what you did to decide if your code is good or not (that is, why there are pull requests, indeed). You could be the best developer in the world. However, if the person at the other end can't get a sense of your commits, your work would probably be refused.

To avoid these unpleasant situations, you have to follow a simple rule: don't do partial commits. If time's up, if you have to go to that damn meeting (programmers hate meetings) or whatever, remember that you can save your work at any moment without committing, using the `git stash` command. If you want to close the commit, because you want to push it to the remote branch for backup purposes, remember that *Git is not a backup tool*. Back up your stash on another disk, put it in the cloud, or simply end your work before leaving, but don't do commits like they are episodes of a TV series.

One more time, Git is a software tool like any other and it can fail. Don't think that just because you are using Git or other versioning systems, you don't need backup strategies. Back up local and remote repositories just like you back up all the other important things.

Describe the change, not what you have done

Too often, I read (and often I wrote) commit messages such as "Removed this", "Changed that", "Added that one", and so on.

Imagine that you are going to work on the common "lost password" feature on your website. Probably, you will find a message like this adequate: "Added the lost password retrieval link to the login page". This kind of commit message does not describe what modifications the feature brings to you, but what you did (and not everything). Try to answer sincerely. If you are reading a repository history, do you want to read what every developer did? Or is it better to read the feature implemented in every single commit?

Try to make the effort, and start writing sentences where the change itself is the subject, not what you did to implement it. Use the imperative present tense (for example, fix, add, implement), describing the change in a small subject sentence, and then, add some details (when needed) in other lines of text. "Implement the password-retrieval mechanism" is a good commit message subject. If you find it useful, then you can add some other information to get a well formed message like this:

```
"Implement the password retrieval mechanism

  - Add the "Lost password?" link into the login page
  - Send an email to the user with a link to renew the password"
```

Have you ever written a changelog for a software by hand? I did; it's one of the most boring things to do. If you don't like writing changelogs, like me, think of the repository history as your changelog. If you take care of your commit messages, you would get a beautiful changelog for free!

In the next section, I will group some other useful hints about good commit messages.

Don't be afraid to commit

Fear is one of the most powerful emotions. It can drive a person to do the craziest thing on Earth. One the most common reactions to fear is breakdown. You don't know what to do, so you end up doing nothing.

This is a common reaction even when you begin to use a new tool such as Git, where gaining confidence can be difficult. For the fear of making a mistake, you don't commit until you are obligated. This is the real mistake; be scared. In Git, you don't have to be scared. Maybe the solution is not obvious; maybe you have to dig on the Internet to find the right way. However, you can get off with small or no consequences, ever (well, unless you are a hard user of the `--hard` option).

On the contrary, you have to make the effort to commit often, as soon as possible. The more frequently you commit, the smaller are your commits; the smaller are your commits, the easier it is to read and understand the changelog. It is also easier to to cherry-pick commits and do code reviews. To help myself get used to committing this way, I followed this simple trick: write the commit message in Visual Studio before starting to write any code.

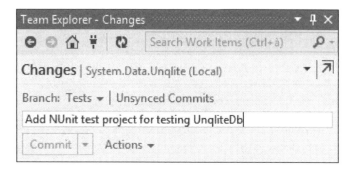

Try to do the same in your IDE or directly in the Bash shell; it helps a lot.

Isolate meaningless commits

The golden rule is to avoid meaningless commits. However, sometimes, you need to commit something that is not a real implementation, but only a cleanup, such as deleting old comments, formatting rearrangement, and so on.

In these cases, it is better to isolate this kind of code change in separate commits. By doing this, you prevent another team member from running towards you with a knife in his hand, frothing at the mouth. Don't commit meaningless changes and mix up them with real ones. Otherwise, other developers (and you, after a couple of weeks) will not understand them while diffing.

The perfect commit message

Let me be honest; the perfect message does not exist. If you work alone, you will probably find the best way for you. However, when in a team, there are different minds and different sensibilities, so what is good for me may not be as good for another.

In this case, you have to sit around a table and discuss. You should try to end up with a shared standard that probably would not be the one you prefer, but at least is a way to start a common path.

Rules for a good commit message really depend on the way you and your team work every day, but some common hints can be applied by everyone. They are described in the following sections.

Writing a meaningful subject

The subject of a commit is the most important part; its role is to make clear what the commit contains. Avoid technical details of other things that a common developer can understand on opening the code. Focus on the big picture. Remember that every commit is a sentence in the repository history. So, wear the hat of the changelog reader and try to write the most convenient sentence for him, not for you. Use the present tense, and write a sentence with a maximum of 50 characters.

A good subject is one like this, "Add the newsletter signup in homepage".

As you can see, I used the imperative past tense. More importantly I didn't say what I have done, but what the feature does: it added a newsletter signup box to my website.

The 50 char rule is due to the way you use Git from the shell or GUI tools. If you start to write long sentences, reviewing logs and so on can become a nightmare. So, don't try to be the Stephen King of commit messages. Avoid adjectives and go straight to the point. You can then write additional details lines.

Another thing to remember is to start with capital letters. Do not end sentences with periods; they are useless and even dangerous.

Adding bulleted details lines, when needed

Often, you can't say all that you want in 50 chars. In this case, use details lines. In this situation, the common rule is to leave a blank line after the subject, use a dash, and go no longer than 72 chars:

```
"Add the newsletter signup in homepage

 - Add textbox and button on homepage
 - Implement email address validation
 - Save email in database"
```

In these lines, add a few details, but not too many. Try to describe the original problem (if you fixed it) or the original need, why these functionalities have been implemented (what problem solves), and understand the possible limitations or issues.

Tie other useful information

If you use some issue and project-tracking systems, write down the issue number, bug IDs or everything else that helps:

```
"Add the newsletter signup in homepage

 - Add textbox and button on homepage
 - Implement email address validation
```

```
- Save email in database

#FEAT-123: closed"
```

Special messages for releases

Another useful thing is to write special format commit messages for releases so that it will be easier to find them. I usually decorate subjects with some special characters, but nothing more. To highlight a particular commit, such as a release one, there is the `git tag` command, remember?

Conclusions

At the end, my suggestion is to try to compose your personal commit message standard by following previous hints, looking at message strategies adopted by great projects and teams around the Web, but especially by doing it. Your standard will change for sure as you evolve as a software developer and Git user. So, start as soon as possible, and let time help you find the perfect way to write a commit message.

At least, don't imitate them: `http://www.commitlogsfromlastnight.com`.

Adopting a workflow – a wise act

Now that you learned how to perform good commits, it's time to fly higher and think about **workflows**. Git is a tool for versioning, but as with other powerful tools, like knives, you can cut tasty sashimi or relieve yourself of some fingers.

The things that separate a great repository from a junkyard are the way you manage releases, the way you react when there is a bug to fix in a particular version of your software, and the way you act when you have to make users beta-test the incoming features.

These kinds of actions belong to ordinary administration for a modern software project. However, very often, I still see teams get out of breath because of the poor versioning workflows.

In this second part of the chapter, we will take a quick look at some of the common workflows alongside the Git versioning system.

Centralized workflows

As we used to do in other VCSes, such as Subversion and so on, even in Git, it is common to adopt a *centralized* way of work. If you work in a team, it is often necessary to share repositories with others, so a common point of contact becomes indispensable.

We can assume that if you are not alone in your office, you would adopt one of the variations of this workflow. As we know, we can get all the computers of our co-workers as remote, in a sort of peer-to-peer configuration. However, you usually don't do this, because it becomes too difficult to keep every branch in every remote in sync.

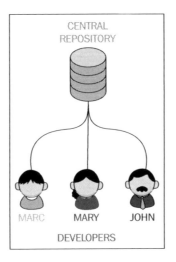

How they work

In this scenario, you usually follow these simple steps:

1. Someone initializes the remote repository (in a local Git server, on GitHub, or on Bitbucket).
2. Other team members clone the original repository on their computer and start working.
3. When the work is done, you push it to the remote to make it available to other colleagues.

At this point, it is only a matter of internal rules and patterns. It is improbable that you and your colleague will work together simultaneously in the master branch, unless you are indomitable masochists.

Feature branch workflow

At this point, you probably will choose a *feature branch* approach, where every single developer works on their branch. When the work is done, the feature branch is ready to be merged with the master branch. You will probably have to merge back from the master branch first because one of your other colleagues has merged a feature branch after you started yours, but after that you basically have finished.

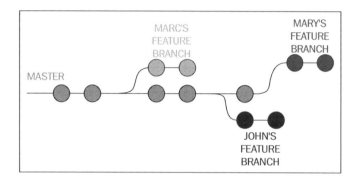

GitFlow

The **GitFlow** workflow comes from the mind of Vincent Driessen, a passionate software developer from the Netherlands. You can find his original blog post at http://nvie.com/posts/a-successful-git-branching-model.

His workflow has gained success over the years, at the point that many other developers (including me), teams and companies started to use it. Atlassian, a well-known company that offers Git related services such as Stash or Bitbucket, integrates the GitFlow directly in its GUI tool, the SourceTree.

Even the GitFlow workflow is a centralized one, and it is well described by this figure:

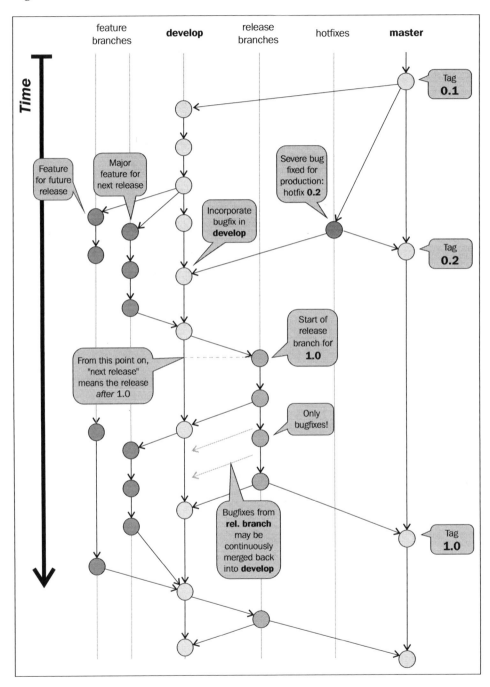

This workflow is based on the use of some **main branches**. What makes these branches special is nothing other than the significance we attribute to them. These are not special branches with special characteristics in Git, but we can certainly use them for different purposes.

The master branch

In GitFlow, the `master` branch represents the final stage. Merging your work in it is equal to making a new release of your software. You usually don't start new branches from the `master` branch. You do it only if there is a severe bug you have to fix instantly, even if that bug has been found and fixed in another evolving branch. This way to operate makes you superfast when you have to react to a painful situation. Other than this, the `master` branch is where you tag your release.

Hotfixes branches

Hotfixes branches are branches derived only from the `master` branch, as we said earlier. Once you have fixed a bug, you merge the `hotfix` branch onto `master` so that you get a new release to ship. If the bug has not been resolved anywhere else in your repository, the strategy would be to merge the `hotfix` branch even into the `develop` branch. After that, you can delete the `hotfix` branch, as it has hit the mark.

In Git, there is a trick to group similar branches: you have to name them using a common prefix followed by a slash /. For the `hotfix` branches, I recommend the `hotfix/<branchName>` prefix (for example `hotfix/LoginBug` of `hotfix/#123` for those who are using bug-tracking systems, where `#123` is the bug ID).

These branches are usually not pushed to remote. You push them only if you need the help of other team members.

The develop branch

The `develop` branch is a sort of *beta software* branch. When you start to implement a new feature, you have to create a new branch starting from the `develop` branch. You will continue to work in that branch until you complete your task.

After the task is completed, you can merge back to the `develop` branch and delete your `feature` branch. Just like `hotfix` branches, these are only temporary branches.

Like the `master` branch, the `develop` branch is a never-ending branch. You will never close nor delete it.

This branch is pushed and shared to a remote Git repository.

The release branch

At some point, you need to wrap up the next release, including some of the features you implemented in the last few weeks. To prepare an incoming release, you have to branch from `develop`, assigning at the branch a name composed of the `release` prefix. This will be followed by the numeric form of your choice for your `release` branch (for example `release/1.0`).

Pay attention. At this stage, no more new features are allowed! You cannot merge `develop` onto the `release` branch. You can only create new branches from that branch for bug fixing. The purpose of this intermediate branch is to give the software to beta testers, allowing them to try it and send you feedback and bug tickets.

If you have fixed some bugs onto the `release` branch, the only thing to remember is to merge them even into the `develop` branch, just to avoid the loss of the bug fix. The `release` branch will not be merged back to `develop`.

You can keep this branch throughout your life, until you decide that the software is both mature and tested sufficiently to go in production. At this point, you merge the `release` branch onto the `master` branch, making, in fact, a new release.

After the merge to `master`, you can make a choice. You could keep the release branch open, if you need to keep alive different releases; otherwise, you can delete it. Personally, I always delete the `release` branch (as Vincent suggests), because I generally do frequent, small, and incremental releases (so, I rarely need to fix an already shipped release). As you certainly remember, you can open a brand new branch from a commit (a tagged one in this case) whenever you want. So, at most, I will open it from that point only when necessary.

This branch is pushed and shared to a common remote repository.

The feature branches

When you have to start the implementation of a new feature, you have to create a new branch from the `develop` branch. Feature branches start with the `feature/` prefix (for example, `feature/NewAuthenitcation` or `feature/#987` if you use some feature- tracking software, as `#987` is the feature ID).

You will work on the feature release until you finish your work. I suggest that you frequently merge back from `develop`. In the case of concurrent modifications to the same files, you will resolve conflicts faster if you resolve them earlier. Then, it is easier to resolve one or two conflicts a time than dozens at the end of the feature work.

Once your work is done, you merge the feature onto `develop` and you are done. You can now delete the `feature` branch.

Feature branches are mainly private branches. However, you could push them to the remote repository if you have to collaborate on it with some other team mates.

Conclusion

I recommend that you take a look at this workflow, as I can assure you that there was never a situation that I failed to solve using this workflow.

You can find a deeper explanation with the ready-to-use Git command on Vincent Driessen's blog. You can even use GitFlow commands Vincent made to customize his Git experience. Check them out on his GitHub account at `https://github.com/nvie/gitflow`.

The GitHub flow

The previously described GitFlow has tons of followers, but it is always a matter of taste. Someone else found it too complex and rigid for their situation. In fact, there are other ways to manage software repositories that have gained consensus during the last few years.

One of these is the workflow used at GitHub for internal projects and repositories. This workflow takes the name of **GitHub flow**. It was first described by the well-known Scott Chacon, former GitHubber and *ProGit* book author, on his blog at `http://scottchacon.com/2011/08/31/github-flow.html`.

This workflow, compared to GitFlow, is better tailored for frequent releases. When I say frequent, I say very frequently, even twice a day. Obviously, this kind of flow works better on web projects, because to deploy it, you have to *only* put the new release on the production server. If you develop desktop solutions, you need a perfect oiled update mechanism to do the same.

GitHub software basically doesn't have releases, because they deploy to production regularly, even more than once a day. This is possible due to a robust **Continuous Delivery** structure, which is not so easy to obtain. It deserves some effort.

The GitHub flow is based on these simple rules.

Anything in the master branch is deployable

Just like GitFlow, even in GitHub flow, deployment is done from the `master` branch. This is the only main branch in this flow. In GitFlow, there are not `hotfix`, `develop`, or other particular branches. Bug fixes, new implementation, and so on are constantly merged onto the `master` branch.

Other than this, code in the `master` branch is always in a deployable state. When you fix or add something new in a branch and then merge it onto the `master` branch, you don't deploy automatically, but you can assume your changes will be up and running in a matter of hours.

Branching and merging constantly to the `master` branch, which is the production-ready branch, can be dangerous. You can easily introduce regressions or bugs, as no one other than you can assure you have done a good job. This problem is avoided by a social contract commonly adopted by GitHub developers. In this contract, you promise to test your code before merging it to the `master` branch, assuring that all automated tests have been successfully completed.

Creating descriptive branches off of the master

In GitFlow, you always branch from the `master` branch. So, it's easy to get a forest of branches to look at when you have to pull one. To better identify them, in GitHub flow, you have to use descriptive names to get meaningful topic branches. Even here, it is a matter of good manners. If you start to create branches named `stuff-to-do`, you would probably fail in adopting this flow. Some examples are `new-user-creation`, `most-starred-repositories`, and so on (note the use of dashes). Using a common way to define topics, you will easily find branches you are interested in, looking for topics' keywords.

Pushing to named branches constantly

Another great difference between GitHub flow and GitFlow is that in GitHub flow, you push feature branches to the remote regularly, even if you are the only developer involved and interested in it. This is done even for backup purposes. Even if I already exposed my opinion in merit, I can't say this is a bad thing.

A thing I appreciate about GitFlow is that this habit of pushing every branch to the remote gives you the ability to see, with a simple `git fetch` command, all the branches currently active. Due to this, you can see all the work in progress, even that of your team mates.

Opening a pull request at any time

In *Chapter 3, Git Fundamentals – Working Remotely*, we talked about GitHub and made a quick try with pull requests. We have seen that basically they are for contributing. You fork someone else's repository, create a new branch, make some modifications, and then ask for a pull request from the original author.

In GitHub flow, you use pull requests massively. You can even ask another developer of your team to have a look at your work and help you, give you a hint, or review the work done. At this point, you can start a discussion about using the GitHub pull request to chat and involve other people, putting their usernames in CC. In addition, the pull request feature lets you comment even a single line of code in a different view, letting users involved proficiently discuss the work under revision.

Merging only after a pull request review

You can now understand that the pull requested branch stage we saw earlier becomes a sort of review stage. Here, other users can take a look at the code and even simply leave a positive comment, just a +1 to make other users know that they are confident about the job, and they approve its merge into `master`.

After this step, when the CI server says that the branch still passes all the automated tests, you are ready to merge the branch in `master`.

Deploying immediately after review

At this stage, you merge your branch into `master`, and the work is done. The deployment is not instantly fired, but at GitHub, they have a very straight and robust deploy procedure. They deploy big branches with 50 commits, but also branches with a single commit and a single line of code change, because deployment is very quick and cheap for them.

This is the reason why they can afford such a simple branching strategy, where you put on the `master` branch, and then you deploy, without the need to pass through the `develop` or `release` stage branch, like in GitFlow.

Conclusions

I consider this flow very responsive and effective for web-based projects, where basically you deploy to production without focusing too much on versions of your software. Using only the `master` branch to derive and integrate branches is faster than light. However, this strategy could be applied only if you have these prerequisites:

- A centralized remote ready to manage pull requests (as GitHub does)
- A good shared agreement about branch names and pull requests usage
- A very robust deploy system

This is a big picture of this flow. For more details, I recommend that you visit the GitHub related page at `https://guides.github.com/introduction/flow/index.html`.

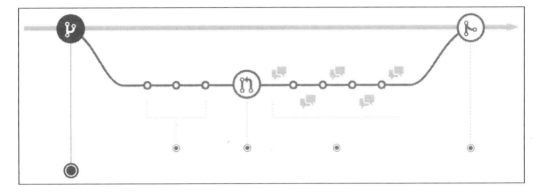

Other workflows

Obviously, there are many other workflows. I will spend just few words on the one that (fortunately) convinced *Linus Torvalds* to realize the Git VCS.

The Linux kernel workflow

The Linux kernel uses a workflow that refers to the traditional way in which *Linus Torvalds* has driven its evolution during these years. It is based on a military-like hierarchy.

Simple kernel developers work on their personal branches, rebasing the `master` branch in the reference repository. Then they push their branches to the lieutenant developer's `master` branch. Lieutenants are developers who *Linus* assigned to particular topics and areas of the kernel because of their experience. When a lieutenants have done their work, they push it to the benevolent dictator `master` branch (**Linus branch**). Then, if things are OK (it is not simple to cheat him), *Linus* would push his `master` branch to the blessed repository, the one that developers use to rebase from, before starting their work.

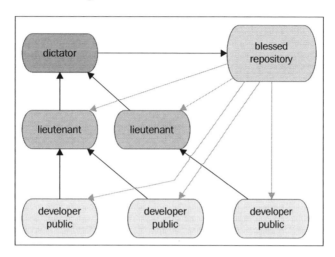

Summary

In this chapter, we became aware of the effective ways to use Git. I personally consider this chapter the most important for a new Git user, because it applies some rules and discipline so that you will obtain the most from this tool. So, pick up a good workflow (make your own, if necessary), and pay attention to your commits. This is the only way to become a good versioning system user, not only in Git.

In the next chapter, we will see some tips and tricks to use Git even if you have to deal with Subversion servers. Then, we will take a quick look at migrating from Subversion to Git.

6
Migrating to Git

In this chapter, we will try to migrate a Subversion repository into a Git one, preserving the changes history. Git and Subversion can coexist as Git has some dedicated commands to exchange data with Subversion, and you can even continue to use both.

The purpose of this chapter is to help developers who actually use Subversion to start using Git instantly, even if the rest of the team continues to use Subversion. In addition, the chapter covers definitive migration for people who decide to abandon Subversion in favor of Git.

Before starting

In the first part of this chapter, we will take a look at some good practices to keep safety and work on actual SVN repository with no hassles. Bear in mind that the purpose of this chapter is only to give readers some hints; dealing with big and complex repositories deserves a more prudent and articulated approach.

Prerequisites

To be able to do these experiments, you need a Subversion tool; on Windows, the most used tool is the well-known **TortoiseSVN** (available at `http://tortoisesvn.net`), which provides both command-line tools: GUI and shell integration.

I recommend to do a full installation of TortoiseSVN, including command-line tools as we'll need some of them to make experiments.

Working on a Subversion repository using Git

In the first part of this chapter, we will see the most cautious approach while starting to move away from Subversion, which is to keep the original repository using Git to fetch and push changes. For the purpose of learning, we will create a local Subversion repository, using both Subversion and Git to access its contents.

Creating a local Subversion repository

Without the hassle of remote servers, let's create a local Subversion repository as a container for our experiments:

```
$ cd \Repos
$ svnadmin create MySvnRepo
```

Now there's nothing more and nothing less to be done here, and the repository is now ready to be filled with folders and files.

Checking out the Subversion repository with svn client

At this point, we have a working Subversion repository; we can now check it out in a folder of our choice, which will become our working copy; in my case, I will use the `C:\Sources` folder:

```
$ cd \Sources\svn
$ svn checkout file:///Repos/MySvnRepo
```

You now have a `MySvnRepo` folder under the `Sources` folder, ready to be filled with your project files; but first let me remind you of a couple of things.

As you may know, a Subversion repository generally has the following subfolder structure:

- `/trunk`: This is the main folder, where generally you have the code under development

- `/tags`: This is the root folder of the snapshots you usually freeze and leave untouched, for example `/tags/v1.0`

- `/branches`: This is the root folder of all the repository branches you will create for feature development, for example `/branches/NewDesign`

Subversion does not provide a command to initialize a repository with this layout (commonly known as **standard layout**), so we have to build it up by hand.

At this point, we can import a skeleton folder that already contains the three subfolders (/trunk, /branches, and /tags) with a command like this:

```
$ cd \Sources\svn\MySvnRepo
$ svn import /path/to/some/skeleton/dir
```

Otherwise, we can create folders by hand using the svn mkdir command:

```
$ cd \Sources\svn\MySvnRepo
$ svn mkdir trunk
$ svn mkdir tags
$ svn mkdir branches
```

Commit the folders we just created and the repository is ready:

```
svn commit -m "Initial layout"
```

Now add and commit the first file, as shown in the following code:

```
$ cd trunk
$ echo "This is a Subversion repo" > readme.txt
$ svn add readme.txt
$ svn commit -m "Readme file"
```

Feel free to add more files or import an existing project if you want to replicate a more real situation; for import files in a Subversion repository, you can use the svn import command, as you saw before:

```
$ svn import \MyProject\Folder
```

Later, we will add a tag and a branch to verify how Git interacts with them.

Cloning a Subversion repository from Git

Git provides a set of tools to cooperate with Subversion; the base command is actually git svn; with git svn you can clone Subversion repositories, retrieve and upload changes, and much more.

So, wear the Git hat and clone the Subversion repository using the git svn clone command:

```
$ cd \Sources\git
$ git svn clone file:///Repos/MySvnRepo
```

`git svn clone` usually runs smoothly on Linux boxes, while in Windows you get a weird error message, as shown here:

```
Couldn't open a repository: Unable to open an ra_local session to URL
```

This happens because in Windows there are some problems in the `git svn` command backport while using the `file://` protocol.

Setting up a local Subversion server

To bypass this problem, we can use the `svn://` protocol instead of `file://`.

To do this, we will use the `svnserve` command to start a Subversion server exposing our repositories directory root. But first we have to edit some files to set up the server.

The main file is the `svnserve.conf` file; look at your `MySvnRepo` repository folder, `C:\Repos\MySvnRepo` in this case, jump into the `conf` subfolder, and edit the file uncommenting these lines (remove the starting #):

```
anon-access = read
auth-access = write
password-db = C:\Repos\MySvnRepo\passwd
authz-db = C:\Repos\MySvnRepo\authz
realm = MySvnRepo
```

Normally, full paths are unnecessary for the `passwd` and `authz` files, but in Windows I find them mandatory, otherwise the Subversion server does not load them.

Now edit the `passwd` file, which contains the user's credentials, and add a new user:

```
[users]
adminUser = adminPassword
```

Then edit the `authz` file and set up groups and rights for the user:

```
[groups]
Admins = admin
```

Continuing with the `authz` file, set rights for repositories; the Admin will have read/write access to all repositories (the section `[/]` means "all repository"):

```
[/]
@Admins = rw
* =
```

At this point, we can start the server with this command:

```
$ svnserve -d --config-file C:\Repos\MySvnRepo\conf\svnserve.conf --root
C:\Repos
```

-d starts the server as a daemon; --config-file specifies the config file to load and --root tells the server where the main root folder of all your repositories is.

Now we have a Subversion server responding at svn://localhost:3690. We can finally clone the repository using Git:

```
$ cd \Sources\git
$ git svn clone svn://localhost/MySvnRepo/trunk
```

This time things will go smoothly; we are now talking with a Subversion server using Git.

Adding a tag and a branch

Just to have a more realistic situation, I will add a tag and a branch; in this manner, we will see how to deal with them in Git.

So, add a new file:

```
$ echo "This is the first file" > svnFile01.txt
$ svn add svnFile01.txt
$ svn commit -m "Add first file"
```

Then tag this snapshot of the repository as v1.0 as you know that in Subversion, a tag or a branch is a copy of a snapshot:

```
$ echo "This is the first file" > svnFile01.txt
$ svn add svnFile01.txt
$ svn copy svn://localhost/MySvnRepo
svn://localhost/MySvnRepo/tags/v1.0 -m "Release 1.0"
```

Committing a file to Subversion using Git as a client

Now that we have a running clone of the original Subversion repository, we can use Git as it was a Subversion client. So add a new file and commit it using Git:

```
$ echo "This file comes from Git" >> gitFile01.txt
$ git add gitFile01.txt
$ git commit -m "Add a file using Git"
```

Now we have to push this file to Subversion:

```
$ git svn dcommit
```

Well done! We can even use Git to fetch changes with the `git svn fetch` command, update the local code using the `git svn rebase` command, and so on; for other commands and options, I recommend that you read the main page of `git svn --help`.

Using Git as a Subversion client is not the best we can obtain, but at least it is a way to start using Git even if you cannot abandon Subversion instantly.

Using Git with a Subversion repository

Using Git as a client of Subversion can raise some confusion due to the flexibility of Git as compared to the more rigid way Subversion organizes files. To be sure to maintain a Subversion-friendly way of work, I recommend that you follow some simple rules.

First of all, be sure your Git `master` branch is related to the `trunk` branch in Subversion; as we already said, Subversion users usually organize a repository in this way:

- a `/trunk` folder, which is the main folder
- a `/branches` root folder, where you put all the branches, each one located in a separate subfolder (for example, `/branches/feat-branch`)
- a `/tags` root folder, where you collect all the tags you made (for example, `/tags/v1.0.0`)

To adhere to this layout, you can use the `--stdlayout` option when you're cloning a Subversion repository:

```
$ git svn clone <url> --stdlayout
```

In this manner, Git will hook the `/trunk` Subversion branch to the Git `master` branch, replicating all the `/branches` and `/tags` branches in your local Git repository and allowing you to work with them in a 1:1 synchronized context.

Migrating a Subversion repository

When possible, it is recommended to completely migrate a Subversion repository to Git; this is quite simple to do and mostly depends on the size of the Subversion repository and the organization.

If the repository follows the standard layout as described before, a migration is only a matter of minutes.

Retrieving the list of Subversion users

If your Subversion repository has been used from different people, you are probably interested in preserving the commit author's name, which is true even in the new Git repository.

If you have the `awk` command available (maybe using Cygwin in Windows), there is a script here that fetches all the users from Subversion logs and appends them to a text file we can use in Git while cloning to perfectly match the Subversion users, even in Git-converted commits:

```
$ svn log -q | awk -F '|' '/^r/ {sub("^ ", "", $2); sub(" $", "", $2);
print $2" = "$2" <"$2">"}' | sort -u > authors.txt
```

Now we will use the `authors.txt` file in the next cloning step.

Cloning the Subversion repository

To begin the migration, we have to locally clone the Subversion repository as we did before; I recommend once more adding the `--stdlayout` option to preserve the branches and tags and then to add the `-A` option to let Git convert commit `authors` while cloning:

```
$ git svn clone <repo-url> --stdlayout --prefix svn/ -A authors.txt
```

In case the Subversion repository has trunks, branches, and tags located in other paths (with no standard layout), Git provides you with a way to specify them with the `--trunk`, `--branches`, and `--tags` options:

```
$ git svn clone <repo-url> --trunk=<trunk-folder> --branches=<branches-
subfolder> --tags=<tags-subfolder>
```

When you fire the `clone` command, remember that this operation can be time-consuming; in a repository with 1000 commits, it is not unusual to wait 15 to 30 minutes for this.

Preserving the ignored file list

To preserve the previously ignored files in Subversion, we can append the `svn:ignore` settings to the `.gitignore` file:

```
$ git svn show-ignore >> .gitignore
```

```
$ git add .gitignore
```

```
$ git commit -m "Convert svn:ignore properties to .gitignore"
```

Pushing to a local bare Git repository

Now that we have a local copy of our repository, we can move it to a brand new Git repository. Here you can already use a remote repository on your server of choice, which can even be GitHub or Bitbucket, but I recommend that you use a local bare repository; we may as well do some other little adjustments (like renaming tags and branches) before pushing files to a blessed repository. So, first initialize a bare repository in a folder of your choice:

```
$ mkdir \Repos\MyGitRepo.git
$ cd \Repos\MyGitRepo.git
$ git init --bare
```

Now make the default branch to match the Subversion `trunk` branch name:

```
$ git symbolic-ref HEAD refs/heads/trunk
```

Then add a `bare` remote pointing to the bare repository just created:

```
$ cd \Sources\MySvnRepo
$ git remote add bare file:///C/Repos/MyGitRepo.git
```

Finally push the local cloned repository to the new bare one:

```
$ git push --all bare
```

We now have a brand new bare repository that is a perfect copy of the original Subversion repository. We can now adjust branches and tags to better fit the usual Git layout.

Arranging branches and tags

Now we can rename branches and tags to obtain a more Git-friendly scenario.

Renaming the trunk branch to master

The Subversion main development branch is /`trunk`, but in Git, as you know, we prefer to call the main branch `master`; here's a way to rename it:

```
$ git branch -m trunk master
```

Converting Subversion tags to Git tags

Subversion treats tags as branches; they are all copies of a certain trunk snapshot. In Git, on the contrary, branches and tags have a different significance.

To convert Subversion tags and branches into Git tags, the following simple script does the work:

```
$ git for-each-ref --format='%(refname)' refs/heads/tags |
cut -d / -f 4 |
while read ref
do
  git tag "$ref" "refs/heads/tags/$ref";
  git branch -D "tags/$ref";
done
```

Pushing the local repository to a remote

You now have a local bare Git repository ready to be pushed to a remote server; the result of the conversion is a full Git repository, where branches, tags, and commit history have been preserved. The only thing you have to do by hand is to eventually accommodate Git users.

Comparing Git and Subversion commands

Here you can find a short and partial recap table, where I try to pair the most common Subversion and Git commands to help Subversion users to quickly shift their minds from Subversion to Git.

Subversion	Git
Creating a repository	
svnadmin create <repo-name> svnadmin import <project-folder>	git init <repo-name> git add . git commit -m "Initial commit"
Getting the whole repository for the first time	
svn checkout <url>	git clone <url>
Inspecting local changes	
svn status svn diff | less	git status git diff

Subversion	Git
Dealing with files (adding, removing, moving)	

`svn add <file>`
`svn rm <file>`
`svn mv <file>`
	`git add <file>`
	`git rm <file>`
	`git mv <file>`

Committing local changes	
`svn commit -m "<message>"`	`git commit -a -m "<message>"`
Reviewing history	
`svn log	less` `svn blame <file>`	`git log` `git blame <file>`
Branching and Tagging	
`svn copy <source> <branch-name>` `svn copy <source> <tag-name>`	`git branch <branch-name>` `git tag -a <tag-name>`
Remember: in Subversion tags and branches represents physical copies of a source branch (the trunk, another branch or another tag), while in Git a tag is only a pointer to a particular commit.	
Merging	
(assuming the branch was created in revision 42 and you are inside a working copy of trunk) `svn merge -r 42:HEAD <branch>`	`git merge <branch>`

Summary

This chapter barely scratches the surface, but I think it'll be useful to get a sense of the topic. If you have wide Subversion repositories, you will probably need better training before starting to convert them to Git, but for small to medium ones, now you know the fundamentals to begin with.

The only suggestion I want to share with you is to not be in a hurry; start by letting Git cooperate with your Subversion server, reorganize your repository when it's messy, do a lot of backups, and finally try to convert it; you will convert it more than once, as I did, but in the end you will get more satisfaction from doing that.

In the next chapter, I will share with you some useful resources I found during my career as a Git user.

7
Git Resources

This chapter is a collection of resources I built during my experience with Git. I will share some thoughts about GUI tools, web interfaces with Git repositories, and learning resources, hoping they will act as a springboard for a successful Git career.

Git GUI clients

When beginning to learn a new tool, especially a wide and complex one like Git, it can be useful to take advantage of some GUI tools that are able to picture commands and patterns in a way that is more simple to understand.

Git benefits from a wide range of GUI tools, so it's only a matter of choice. I want to tell you right away that there is no perfect tool, as frequently happens, but there are enough of them to pick the one that fits your needs better.

Windows

As a Microsoft .NET developer, I use Windows 99 percent of the time. In spare time, I play a little bit with Linux, but in that case I prefer to use the command line. In this section, you will find tools I use or I have used in the past, while in the other platform section I will provide only some hints based on words of other people.

Git GUI

Git has an integrated GUI, as we learnt from the previous chapters. Probably, it is not one of the most eye-catching solution you will find, but for small issues it can be enough. The reason for using it is that it is already installed when you install Git, and that it is well integrated even with the command prompt; so for blaming files, see history or interactive merging can be fired easily (just type `git gui <command>` on your shell). But I have to come clean: I don't like it much.

In Windows, Git GUI will be installed following the language or the region you specified on Windows. What's the problem? Well, the problem is that in non-English languages, they translate everything - even command names! In Italian, instead of merge I see **Fusione**; pushing gets translated as **Propaga;** and untracked files become **Modifiche non preparate**. The problem is not the translation itself, but simply that I find translating concepts or command names (like even Windows and other Microsoft tools did in the past) perplexing; it is confusing and counterproductive.

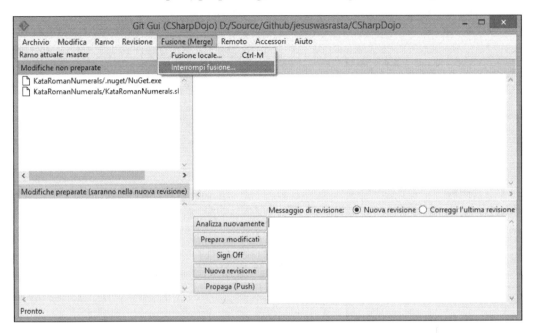

TortoiseGit

If you have migrated from using Subversion to using Git, you have probably already heard about **TortoiseSVN**, a well-crafted tool for dealing with Subversion commands directly from Explorer, through the right-click shell integration.

TortoiseGit brings Git, instead of Subversion, to the same place. By installing TortoiseGit, you will benefit from the same Explorer integration, leaving most Git commands only a step away from you. Even if I discourage you to use localized versions, TortoiseGit is available in different languages. Also, bear in mind that you need to install Git in advance as it is not included in the TortoiseGit setup package.

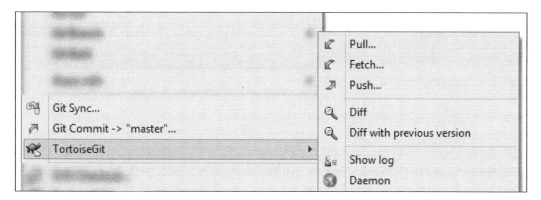

GitHub for Windows

GitHub offers a stylish Modern UI based client. I have to admit that I snubbed it at first, mostly because I was sure that I could use it only for GitHub repositories. However, I realized that one can use it even with other remotes, but it's clear that the client is tailored for GitHub. To use other remotes, you have to edit the config file by hand, substituting the GitHub remote with the one you want.

If you want a general purpose client, probably this is not the best tool for you; but if you work mostly on GitHub, it may likely be the best GUI in the market.

Atlassian SourceTree

This is my favorite client. SourceTree is free like all the other tools; it comes from the mind of Atlassian, the well-known company behind Bitbucket and other popular services like Jira, Confluence, and Stash. SourceTree can handle all kinds of remotes, offering facilities (like remembering passwords) to access the most popular services like Bitbucket and GitHub.

It embeds the GitFlow way of organizing repositories by design, offering a convenient button to initialize a repository with GitFlow branches, and integrating GitFlow commands provided by the author. The most interesting thing I found at first was that you can enable a window where SourceTree shows the equivalent Git command when you use some of Git commands by user interface; in this manner, when you doubt you can remember the right command for the job, you can use SourceTree to accomplish your task and see what commands it uses to get the work done.

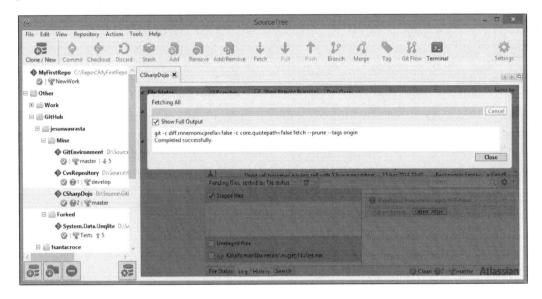

SourceTree is available even for Mac OS X.

Cmder

Cmder is not really a Git GUI, but a nicer portable console emulator you can use instead of the classic Bash shell:

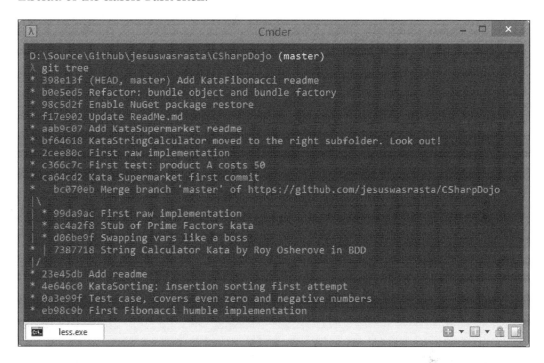

It looks nicer than the original shell; it has multi-tab support and a wide set of configuration options to let you customize it as you prefer, thanks to ConEmu and Clink projects. Finally yet importantly, it comes with Git embedded. You can download it from GitHub at `https://github.com/bliker/cmder`.

Mac OS X

As I already said, I have no experience with Mac OS X Git clients; the only information I can share with you is that GitHub offers its client for free, even for Mac, like it does Atlassian with SourceTree. There is no TortoiseGit for Mac, but I have heard about a cool app called Git Tower. Please consider giving it a try as it seems very well crafted.

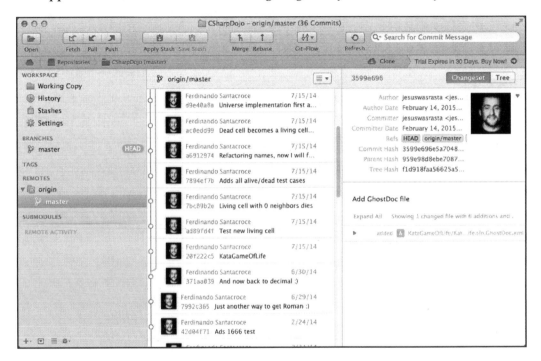

Another great tool is SmartGit, available for free for open-source projects: http://www.syntevo.com/smartgit/

Linux

Linux is the reason for Git, so I think that it is the best place to work with Git. I play with Linux now and then, and I usually use the Bash shell for Git.

For the ZSH shell lover, I suggest looking at http://ohmyz.sh/, an interesting open source project where you can find tons of plugins and themes. About plugins, there are some of them that let you enhance your Git experience with this famous alternate console.

You can take a look at some Git GUI for Linux at

http://git-scm.com/download/gui/linux

Building up a personal Git server with web interface

In the office where I work, I was the first person who started to use Git for production code. At some point, after months of little trials in my spare time, I gained courage and converted all the Subversion repositories, where I usually work alone, into Git ones.

Unfortunately, firm IT policies forbid me to use external source code repositories; so no GitHub or Bitbucket. To make things even worse, I also could not obtain a Linux server, and take advantage of great web interfaces like Gitosis, GitLab, and so on. So I started to Google around the web for a solution, and I finally found a solution that can be useful for people in a similar condition.

The SCM Manager

SCM Manager (`https://www.scm-manager.org/`) is a very easy solution to share your Git repositories in a local Windows network. It offers a standalone solution to install and make it work on top of Apache Web Server directly in Windows. Though it is built in Java, you can make it work even in Linux or Mac.

It can manage Subversion, Git, and Mercurial repositories, allowing you to define users, groups, and so on. It has a good list of plugins too for other version control systems and other development related tools like Jenkins, Bamboo, and so on. There's also a Gravatar plugin and an Active Directory plugin, to let you and other colleagues use default domain credentials to access your internal repositories.

I've been using this solution for about two years without a hitch, excluding only some configuration related annoyances during updates, due to my custom path personalization.

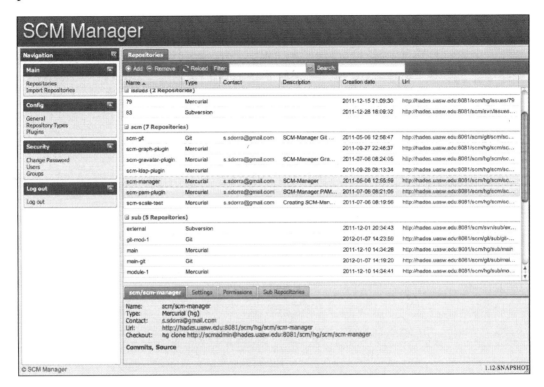

Learning Git in a visual manner

The last thing I would like to share with readers is a web app I found useful at the very beginning, to better understand the way Git works.

LearnGitBranching (`http://pcottle.github.io/learnGitBranching/`) is a tremendously helpful web app that offers you some exercises to help you grow your Git culture. Starting from basic commit exercises, you learn how to branch, rebase, and so on. However, the really cool thing is that at the right side of the page, you will see a funny repository graph evolving in real time, following the commands you type in the emulated shell.

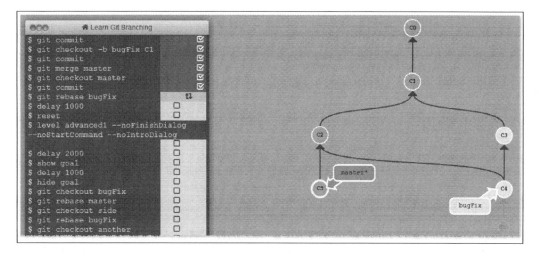

Git on the Internet

In the end, I would suggest you to follow some resources that I usually follow to learn new things and get in touch with other smart and funny Git users over the Internet.

Git community on Google+

This community is full of people who are happy to share their knowledge with you; most of the coolest things I know about Git have been discovered here, at:

```
https://plus.google.com/u/0/communities/112688280189071733518
```

GitMinutes and Thomas Ferris Nicolaisen's blog

Thomas is a skilled Git user, and a very kind person. On his blog, you will find many interesting resources, including videos where he talks about Git at local German programming events.

More than this, Thomas runs GitMinutes podcast series, where he talks about Git with other people, discussing general purpose topics, tools opinions, and so on.

Take a look at www.tfnico.com and www.gitminutes.com.

Ferdinando Santacroce's blog

On my personal blog, http://jesuswasrasta.com/, I recently started a *Git Pills* series, where I share with readers some things I discovered using Git, quick techniques to get the job done, and how to recover from weird situations.

Summary

In this chapter, we went through some Git GUI clients. Even if I encourage people to understand Git by using shell commands, I have to admit that for most common tasks, using a GUI based tool makes me feel more comfortable, especially when diffing or reviewing history.

Then we discovered that we could obtain a personal Git server with a fancy web interface: the Internet has plenty of good pieces of software to achieve this target.

At the end, like my last suggestion, I mentioned some good resources to enhance your Git comprehension: all the knowledge fields, hearing the voice of the experts, and asking them questions is the most effective way to get your work done.

Index

svn client
Subversion repository, checking
out with 116, 117
symbolic references 86
system-wide configurations 76

T

Team Foundation Server (TFS) 1
tilde character 86
time metaphor
about 17
future 21
past 17, 18
present 18-20
TortoiseGit 126
TortoiseSVN
about 126
URL 115
tricks
about 92
bare repositories 92
typos 79

U

user-wide configurations 77

V

Version Control System (VCS) 96
Vim (Vi Improved) 10
visual diff tool
using 43
visual manner
Git, learning in 132

W

web interface
personal Git server, building with 131
Windows 125
workflows
adopting 103
centralized workflows 104
feature branch workflow 105
working directory
about 13
file statuses 14
world-wide techniques
about 88
changes, tracing in file 88-90
cherry picking activity 90, 91
last commit message, modifying 88

Thank you for buying
Git Essentials

About Packt Publishing

Packt, pronounced 'packed', published its first book, *Mastering phpMyAdmin for Effective MySQL Management*, in April 2004, and subsequently continued to specialize in publishing highly focused books on specific technologies and solutions.

Our books and publications share the experiences of your fellow IT professionals in adapting and customizing today's systems, applications, and frameworks. Our solution-based books give you the knowledge and power to customize the software and technologies you're using to get the job done. Packt books are more specific and less general than the IT books you have seen in the past. Our unique business model allows us to bring you more focused information, giving you more of what you need to know, and less of what you don't.

Packt is a modern yet unique publishing company that focuses on producing quality, cutting-edge books for communities of developers, administrators, and newbies alike. For more information, please visit our website at www.packtpub.com.

About Packt Open Source

In 2010, Packt launched two new brands, Packt Open Source and Packt Enterprise, in order to continue its focus on specialization. This book is part of the Packt Open Source brand, home to books published on software built around open source licenses, and offering information to anybody from advanced developers to budding web designers. The Open Source brand also runs Packt's Open Source Royalty Scheme, by which Packt gives a royalty to each open source project about whose software a book is sold.

Writing for Packt

We welcome all inquiries from people who are interested in authoring. Book proposals should be sent to author@packtpub.com. If your book idea is still at an early stage and you would like to discuss it first before writing a formal book proposal, then please contact us; one of our commissioning editors will get in touch with you.

We're not just looking for published authors; if you have strong technical skills but no writing experience, our experienced editors can help you develop a writing career, or simply get some additional reward for your expertise.

PUBLISHING

Git Version Control Cookbook

ISBN: 978-1-78216-845-4   Paperback: 340 pages

90 hands-on recipes that will increase your productivity when using Git as a version control system

1. Filled with practical recipes that will teach you how to use the most advanced features of the Git system.

2. Improve your productivity by learning to work faster, more efficiently, and with more confidence.

3. Discover tips and tricks that will show you when and how to use the advanced features of Git.

Mastering Git [Video]

ISBN: 978-1-78355-413-3   Duration: 01:49 hours

Manage your projects with the aid of hands-on exercises that make Git easy for you

1. Expand your confidence with Git and gain a better understanding of how it works for easier Source Control Management.

2. Have a smooth and effortless coding experience with features such as Stash, Aliases, and more.

3. Go beyond the command line, and enjoy the benefits of GUI clients for Git.

Please check **www.PacktPub.com** for information on our titles

GitLab Cookbook

ISBN: 978-1-78398-684-2   Paperback: 172 pages

Over 60 hands-on recipes to efficiently self-host your own Git repository using GitLab

1. Get hands-on with day-to-day tasks to effectively manage and administer your repository with GitLab.

2. Covers advanced topics like GitLab continuous integration and LDAP integration.

3. Authored by a member of the GitLab core team, this Cookbook gives practical insights into installing and self-hosting your own GitLab and GitLab CI server.

Git Best Practices Guide

ISBN: 978-1-78355-373-0   Paperback: 102 pages

Master the best practices of Git with the help of real-time scenarios to maximize team efficiency and workflow

1. Work with a versioning tool for continuous integration using Git.

2. Learn how to make the best use of Git's features.

3. Comprehensible guidelines with useful tricks and tips for effectively using Git for collaborative and Agile development.

Please check **www.PacktPub.com** for information on our titles